"The present should interpret
the past, purely and clearly,
so that the future will understand
and be inspired by it."
— Sven Grundtvig
Danish folklorist

Notes From a Scandinavian Parlor

by Florence Ekstrand

Illustrations by
Kris Ekstrand Molesworth

Cover panel: From a folk painting
by Johannes Nilsson (1757-1827),
"The Wedding in Cana." In the
Varberg Museum.

Published by

Welcome
Press

2701 Queen Anne
Avenue North
Seattle, Washington
98109

*To Nathaniel,
Andrew and Claire, and
to their Papa Morry, who
would have approved.*

Besides the people mentioned in this book and others who in one way or another encouraged the writing of it, I want to say a special "Thanks!" to Professor Arne Pederson of Pacific Lutheran University; Professor Birgitta Steen of the University of Washington; Marianne Forssblad of the Nordic Heritage Museum and Edward D. Egerdahl of the Scandinavian Language Institute, both of Seattle, Washington; Bodil Bak Jones of Seattle's Danish Trade Office; Rod MacAdam of Kilmarnock, Ayrshire, who knows the Viking past; Jack Tibbets of Ketchikan, Alaska, and Margaret Leuthner of Alexandria, Minnesota, who, we hope, will soon write the story of the Kensington Stone.

Introduction

In the Minnesota farmhouse where I grew up there was a big blue enamel range with a hot water reservoir and a teakettle that steamed and sang. There was a wood and coal-gobbling furnace in the basement with radiators that hissed and pinged their way through the winter. There was a glassed-in front porch where I cut paper dolls through the summer and where the Christmas sausage and sylta lay frozen in icy crocks in December. There was a parlor with lace curtains and an oak parlor table and black leather furniture and a huge fern.

And a reed organ.

Why we had an organ I have no idea. No one played it.

Let me restate that. I played it.

I had a repertoire of two tunes: "Peter, Peter, Pumpkin Eater" on the black keys and something called "Goobenooah" on the white keys. My brother Ernie taught them to me. They were his whole repertoire, too. I could play them today.

But it has taken me most of a lifetime to learn that "Goobenooah," that funny little two-finger tune I played, is actually a song with words, an ages-old Swedish folk song. A song of many verses, dealing with "Old Man Noah," it was sung by country people in the days when they gathered for threshing bees or when the young people came together for the first spring day in the woods.

For many of us, our Scandinavian heritage and family traditions are a little like the song about "Gubben Noah." We practice them but we don't know why. We know we have roots in the far past but we aren't sure what they are. We bake rosettes at Christmas and dust them with powdered sugar because "Grandma always did." We hang a sheaf of grain for the birds and wonder how the custom began. We admire brightly painted woodenware at an exhibit and dream of who may first have painted those glowing flowers and graceful swirls. We sense vague yearnings to be united with a specific past. We long for some tie with a forefather or foremother who watched the fierce North Sea batter a rocky coast. But we're not sure what is there, nor how we may become part of it.

In short, we play the tune but we don't know the words.

This book is for you who play the tune. And if in it you should find the words, if it sheds some light on who we Scandinavians are and how we became what we are, then both you and I will be happy.

And you needn't be Scandinavian! If there is a richness in the traditions of the north countries, if there is a custom that warms the spirit or brightens a gathering, then adopt it and enjoy!

No book like this can be done without a certain bias. Our past is interpreted — perhaps even colored — by our own point of view. Mine is that of a second generation Swedish American sprung for the most part from peasant stock — small farmers, cotters, hired hands in the southern provinces. For that reason, emphasis here is on the life and arts of the common people as these have come down to us. To explore the more sophisticated arts and culture, in which the Scandinavian countries richly abound, you'll find a wealth of sources. And your search will be just as enjoyable and rewarding as this one has been.

1.

The Vikings

We are not descended from saints

To take a liking to a Viking is not easy.

The Arabs called them *madjus,* which means "heathen monsters." A French litany of the time petitioned God for "deliverance from the fury of the Norsemen" and their indiscriminate throat-cutting. The far-roaming Norsemen collected human booty and set up slave markets. Any coastal settlement was fair game.

And when they raided Lindisfarne, near the east coast of Northumbria, burning, robbing and pillaging, the gentle Celtic monks who survived to record the event and exact date (June 9, 793) noted that their coming was preceded by all kinds of signs — whirlwinds, comets and famine.

We are not descended from saints.

And yet for about two centuries they left their mark on a world that was ahead of them in civilized ways. The Vikings were mad about boats and made use of the sea as no people before them had done. They developed trade and with it came changes in almost every way of life, especially in their homelands. New land was opened for cultivation. The iron craftsmanship that made the warrior vessels strong brought better plows to till their heavy soils for growing rye. Trading led to the establishment of new towns and the beginnings of a merchant class.

~~~~~~

About 200 people now live in Lindisfarne, the "Holy Island" of England. It is near the Scottish border and may be reached either by ferry or a causeway that is open only at low tide. The gold-illuminated manuscripts which were produced here by Celtic monks in the 7th century are safe in the British Museum in London. When the marauding Vikings finally forced the surviving monks to flee inland, they established the city of Durham but eventually returned to Lindisfarne. But Henry III's Dissolution Act halted the work of the monks on the island. Now the ruins of the priory and castle are a tourist attraction.

~~~~~~

But the Vikings, taking to their ships from roughly the 700s to almost 1000, were not the first "northmen."

They came from the south, those first hardy souls venturing into an unknown north. Remains found along receding coastal waters show that a migratory people had survived along the Baltic Sea even before the beginning of the fifth millenium, when increasing warmth was causing ice to melt and form the great sea channels. Some time after 2000 B.C., there are indications of a new wave of nomads who rode horses, probably bringing them from the area around the Black Sea. By the Bronze Age (about 1500-500 B.C.) Denmark and southern Sweden were felling the forests, working in metal alloys, weaving textiles and importing finished objects like bronze swords.

The civilized world of that time paid little attention to this far northern area until about the third century B.C. Even when explorers and early geographers recorded their impressions of the long hours of daylight during the summer, the crops that were grown and the weather (which was in a colder, wetter cycle than for the previous 2000 years), no one was much interested. For lack of written accounts, information about the north lands during the period of the Great Migrations and the breakup of the Roman Empire must depend largely on archaeological finds made in later years. And in the late eighth century, when Charlemagne was building his empire on Christian foundations, no one saw the land of the Svear or Saevo people as attracting any more attention than a very moderate trade by sea.

But the Scandinavians were learning to build light, fleet boats manned by as many as 20 and 24 oarsmen. And when the time was right, when the need was at its keenest and the motivation overpowering, they made themselves known.

~~~~~~

Some early historians wasted few words on the Vikings. In one case, the Anglo-Saxon Chronicle, reporting on a naval armament invading Ireland, summed it up curtly: "It is tedious to tell how it all fell out."

~~~~~~

The name Viking may have come from the Latin *vicus,* meaning a place, a market place, a village. More likely it is derived from the Scandinavian vik, a small bay or inlet. "Men of the creeks," some called them. Others say the name could have meant "sea warrior on a long voyage from home." They were called normanni, or Norsemen (Northmen). The Slavic word for them was rus, after the Swedish *ruotsi,* or "oarsmen." Russians referred to them as "Varangians."

Who knows what the coastal people as far south as the Mediterranean called them? They knew only that these incredibly swift boats came from a forbidding north world locked in ice and snow and brooding black forests. The raids were accomplished swiftly. The small crews depended on surprise. There must not be time to muster a defense. Kill whatever it is necessary to kill, make a quick foray, load the spoils into the boat that has been dragged up on shore, torch the buildings and either raise the sail or man the oars. When their force was large enough or the devastated area unpopulated enough, the invaders might settle in, gain lands for themselves, take wives from the area and eventually impart to the area the flavor of their own Viking culture.

The hunger for land launched many a Viking ship. But even a landed man, a farmer with fields and family, would leave it all in the care of his wife and a few trusted freedmen and slaves and join a raiding foray that might last a year or two. For him there was always the dream of spoils to divide: gold and silver chains to add to his stature as a manor owner, tankards for his table, swords and spears to be buried with him when he died.

But as much as land and spoils, the lust for adventure stirred them. It was a life to be savored and to be talked over and retold for years in their

11

dark and smoky *stues*. They were the first of their time to sail the open ocean. The coastlines of western Europe were open or closed to them depending on how strong were those kingdoms at the time. Although they ranged far south, large areas of the Mediterranean were closed to them because of the military might of the Arabs. But in the far southeast, at the mouth of the Volga, they were able to make contact peacefully enough with Arab traders.

But the Atlantic was always before them. Since surprise was such an important element, Viking raiders picked islands with level, shallow beaches on which to make a first attack and often establish headquarters. Not only could they jump out and attack quickly, but larger ships pursuing them

When Napoleon had finished reading The Iliad, he made a comment that might well have been applied to the Vikings as well: "I am especially struck by the rude manners of the heroes, as compared with their lofty thoughts."

would get hung up on the shoals.

Early in the 800s, raiders largely from Norway reached the Hebrides and the Scottish mainland. In 836 Viking bands made a swift, plundering expedition on the Irish coast and fortified the place. Because the Irish had long been Christians, there were rich monasteries, many of them already seats of learning. On the first raids the Norsemen were after cattle, slaves and booty, even to the plundering of graves. Most horrifying to the Irish was the plundering of sacred books, vessels, croziers and other objects in the churches themselves. (And there was some strange behavior when the "infidels" settled down on this coast for good; one Norseman, Thorgist, emptied the church's coffers into his own and then set himself up as the Abbot of Armagh with his wife as abbotess!)

Although they never conquered inland Ireland, it was from the Irish coast that they made their way eastward through northwest England. Islands at the mouth of the Thames — Thanet, Mersea and Sheppey — became bases for their attacks on England's east coast. From here in the middle of the 9th century they moved north to Northumberland, where they exploited a current civil war, gained a foothold and stayed. Their leader, Halfdan, distributed land to his Danish men, and both here and in the York area the community came to be stamped with Danish customs and Nordic-type law. These people were farmers at heart and they settled gradually into the land and were assimilated into it. In the 10th century, when the Danelaw (the area under Danish law) was repossessed by the Anglo-Saxons, there was no indication that the Scandinavians suffered any reprisals.

Viking Tools. 1179.

In 1958 on St. Ninians in the Shetland Islands, a rich hoard of treasure was found under a slab of sandstone in a church: seven silver bowls, a larchwood box, a spoon, a pommel for the hilt of a sword, two horseshoe-like mountings and 12 brooches. These had likely been hidden from the Vikings, who began to appear around the Shetlands by 850. Some settled there for good. The soil was fertile for cattle-raising and fishing was good. They built their houses as they had built at home, with low stone walls and saddle roofs. Usually there would be one longhouse and several outbuildings. Similar houses may be seen in the Hebrides. Many finds in the Shetlands date to the 9th century — spear tips, combs, bone pins, vessels and spindle-whorls of the native soapstone.

Nor were Iceland and the Faroe Islands too far out in the Atlantic to be overlooked. Viking sailors on their way to Ireland made assaults on the Faroes until the Celtic monks fled the islands in about 800. The capitol of the Faroes, Torshavn ("Thor's haven"), began as the central gathering place for the invaders and new settlers. And the fine wools of these islands had their start in the sheep which those early Norwegian seafarers brought with them in their boats.

Because Iceland was colonized so early in history and its meagre population so isolated, its origins of government go back further in time than those of any similarly constituted European state. Here, too, is the first written history of this era; passages of reminiscing in some of Iceland's heroic poems provide the nearest thing we have to written history of the Viking exploits. The first permanent settlers came from Norway around 874.

By the time Erik the Red and his son Leif came on the scene some hundred years later, the age of the Vikings was yielding to the age of settlement.

During the earlier half of the Viking period, while distinctions between the three northern countries were becoming more clear, and while the Danes and Norwegians were venturing further to the west, Swedish bands were traveling east. They did little colonizing; the fact that they called Russia Gardarike ("land of settlements") indicates that large trade settlements were already there. While the Swedes were most interested in trade routes, they found opportunities to plunder along the Black Sea and across the Caspian. The profits from both the trading and plundering are reflected in the large numbers of Arabian coins found in the treasures of the Vikings.

How they must have loved their boats! Fortunately for us, we may see these "steeds of the sea" not only in carvings on ancient rune stones but in several well-preserved ships raised from sea bottoms or land graves where kings and queens were buried in them.

Two of the best known of the unearthed Viking ships are the Gokstad ship found in 1880 and the Oseberg ship found in 1904. Both are in the Ship Museum in Bygdoy near Oslo. The Oseberg ship had in it the skeletons of two women and is believed to have been the burial ship of Queen Asa of Norway, with her servant. Because of the elaborate carving on the ship, the bones of horses, dogs and oxen around it and the wealth of household items in it — even sleighs, a cart and framework for a small house, this find has yielded much information about Viking life. Ships and fragments of ships have been found in all three Scandinavian countries.

Unlike the Roman sailing vessels, built for use on the calm Mediterranean, the earliest Viking ships had neither sail nor keel but were powered by men at oars. The development of sail and keel was a great forward step and must have come after much trial and error, for in boats as small as theirs balance was all-important. The ships had to be broad to carry as many men and provisions as possible. But they must be able to cut through huge waves and ride out gales on the Atlantic and Baltic Seas, and so easily maneuvered that they could pull up on a beach almost unannounced.

(Not all their ships were small. One tale tells of the building of the Long Serpent near Trondheim in 998. It had 32 or 34 pair of oars, making it possibly 120 feet long. And of the five Viking ships raised from Roskilde Fjord in Denmark in 1968, the largest is 95 feet long and could have carried 50 to 60 men. Two of these are cargo ships, broader and deeper than the others.)

Whatever navigational equipment they could have had was of the crudest kind. Likely they depended most on sun and stars and the movement of sea birds and sea creatures. How far did they sail? No one knows for sure, but Chinese silk was found in Viking graves at Birka, and on Lake Malor in Sweden archaeologists found a perfect small Buddha seated on a lotus flower!

~~~~~~

The nursery rhyme, "London Bridge is falling down," is believed to have originated in the story of Olaf Tryggvesson, a Norse king who founded Trondheim in 997. On one of his harrying expeditions overseas, he sailed up the Thames to London Bridge, put ropes around the piles, fastened them to his ships and sailed downstream. The bridge burst and many are said to have drowned.

~~~~~~

During the two hundred years that these Northmen terrorized the Christian and pagan world, life was changing at home. Small cultivated areas were being carved out of the forest. Farmhouses, their size depending on the wealth and status of their owners, were soon surrounded by fields and meadows.

Since that "wealth and status" dictated lifestyle so sharply even then, it's difficult to describe the life of a "typical" Viking. The Vikings liked to profess that they were all equal. But runestones and graves speak clearly of kings, chieftans, free warriors, smiths, ship-owners, women (as a class), freedmen and slaves. Life differed depending on whether the head of the

15

household was a king, a commander, an administrator of the king's estates, an earl (provincial ruler) or a farmer. And while it differed even more for the slaves, of which a large landowner might have 50 to 100, tradition guaranteed a certain amount of fair treatment for slaves and good standing for freedmen.

Ownership of land was all-important. Farms were scattered up and down the valleys. The large landowner had a "great hall" in which to eat and entertain. The ordinary small farmer likely had a rectangular house with an open hearth in the center, low bunks along the wall, and the domestic animals housed at one end — a renewable heat source! In the far north areas, turf and stone were piled as an outer embankment around a timber house. Many were covered with wattle and daub, clay applied in a thick layer over a sort of plait-work covering the walls. Roofs were of straw or turf.

Crops like barley, rye, wheat, oats, peas and onions are mentioned early in Viking times. Relics from the Iron Age indicate that even then grain was being roasted before it was ground. It also seems that as far back as the Viking Age, farmers increased the fertility of their soil by letting it lie fallow and manuring it. Also, if one could rotate between a winter crop, a summer crop and lying fallow, one made sure of a yield each year. Sledges found among the Oseberg remains might have been used for carrying dung to the fields, with slaves providing the manpower.

In other ways than farming these people adapted to the conditions where they lived. On the thousands of islands they caught birds and gathered birds' eggs. Birds provided more than food: a quilt found in the Oseberg grave was filled with bird feathers, as are other quilts found in rich graves. Some quarried soapstone and bog iron. Near as they were to the sea, there was always fishing.

But none of these things occupied all their time. When things had been quiet too long, the sleek boat with the carved prow would be fitted and provisioned again. And on a biting cold dawn, oars would dip in the black water again and blood would race through the veins in a frenzy of anticipation.

It was at times like these that the woman of the manor came into her own. Like the farm wife of today, she was always a vital part of the operation; though there might be slaves and sons' wives to help, the responsibility for feeding and clothing a household that might run over a hundred in all essentially fell on her. She saw to it that enough rye was safely stored for winter bread, that fish was dried and meat salted and smoked, and that the spinning and weaving kept up with the growing need.

And when her husband sailed off for what might be anything from a couple of months to years, she became "keeper of the keys." Literally she carried on a belt around her waist the keys to the family storehouses that held everything from dried venison to gold pieces left from the last plundering. Hers was the only authority to say what could be taken and what must be left. She became, in effect, the head of the manor.

16

The Oseberg Ship
Viking Ships Museum.
Oslo.

Imprint on England

The imprint of the early Scandinavians on what would in time become England, Ireland and Scotland was more than language similarities and place names (all the English "gate" suffixes come from the Scandinavian *gata* — "street").

It started long before the Danish Vikings headed into the sea. For centuries other invaders had entered the islands, conquered, and been themselves conquered by new invaders — Celts, Iberians, Romans, Saxons.

But historian George Macaulay Trevelyan calls the settlement of the Nordic people in the islands the "governing event of British history." By "Nordic" he refers to the scattered tribes of Scandinavians, Anglo-Saxons, Franks and Teutons who more or less established the racial character of the country.

In the 9th century, while the Swedish Vikings were harrying Slav territories and Constantinople, the Danes were attacking both sides of what would be known as the English Channel. As a result two "Dane-laws," areas ruled by Danes, were carved out. One, carved out of the Frankish kingdom on the east shores of the channel, came to be called Normandy for the "north men." The other took in all of eastern England.

The English learned from the Danes how to build walls around their cities and how to build earthen forts to house their garrisons. The Danes that settled in owned no slaves and lived peacably once they had the land they wanted. In fact, they had little sympathy for the Viking raids that continued for well another century after the Danelaw. The continued hammering of those Danes forced English kings to arm their nobles and their vassals, hastening the move from a tribal culture to the feudal culture of the middle ages.

On the other hand, the Viking raids set back for perhaps a century the "civilizing" of the isles. The churches, repositories of learning, were plundered and destroyed. The priests and monks, who were the scholars, were killed or driven away. In the time of Alfred the Great, the clergy still said Mass but could no longer understand the Latin they chanted.

At last, in 1016, following bloody warfare, the Saxons picked Canute of Denmark to be their king. Trade began to flourish and Danish citizens became leading citizens of London. Careful to put Danes and English on an equal footing, Canute gained the support of all.

And when, 50 years later, the Normans crossed the channel and conquered, it was a people with both Scandinavian and French blood and culture that poured into England. The tremendous energy of the Vikings, their vigor, their ability to adapt, all would become the backbone of Norman feudalism and the beginnings of structured government for the English.

18

Hagar, a lovable Viking

There IS a lovable Viking.

At least, readers of 1400 newspapers worldwide have taken him into their hearts.

Dik Browne, 65, started drawing Hagar the Horrible in 1973 and the ferocious, marauding Viking (who has all our own faults and foibles) ranks among the most popular comic strips today.

Browne had done the drawing for the "Hi and Lois" strip since 1954.

"But," said Browne, "I wanted to do a new strip with a completely new character. I wanted him to be instantly recognizable, a free soul, who could be put into a variety of situations, and HAGAR seemed to appear magically before me as if to say, 'That's me!' "

Browne says he's been in love with Vikings ever since he was quite small.

Vikings, he thinks, must have had good public relations.

"Some years ago I had Attila the Hun saying to Hagar, 'You Vikings do the same things we Huns do. But does anybody hate you? Nooooo. How come?' And Hagar simply replied, 'Class!' "

The visit with Hagar on these pages is reprinted with the permission of King Features Syndicate, Inc.

Fly the Flags!

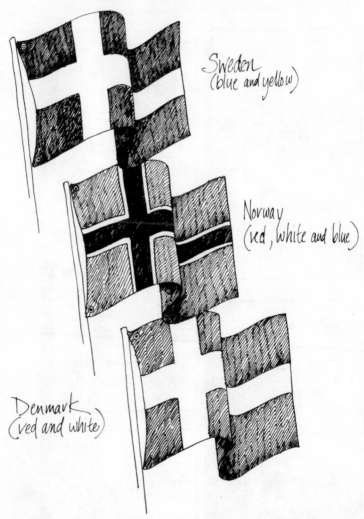

Sweden
(blue and yellow)

Norway
(red, white and blue)

Denmark
(red and white)

Here we tend to fly the flag on holidays only, while Scandinavians are more likely to fly theirs every day. However, if you wish to fly the two flags on holidays, here are some you might observe: Norwegian Constitution Day, May 17; Danish Constitution Day, June 5; Swedish Flag Day, June 6; Midsummer Day (all Scandinavian countries), and of course our own legal holidays. Scandinavians also fly their flags on birthdays of royal family members.

2.

An Abbreviated History

In no other country than the United States is the question asked so often: "What nationality are you?" or "What nationality is your name?"

Those of us with Nordic lineage say "Swedish" or "Norwegian" or "Danish" or whatever.

But my parents came from southern Sweden. That area was long under Danish rule. Am I then of Danish background?

Questions like this and the mixed parentage that often includes ALL the Scandinavian lines make it easy to say simply, "I'm Scandinavian." After all, the north countries are more of a cultural entity than any other group of European nations. Languages are quite similar. (True, many Swedes and Danes may not understand each other, but then some Swedes, Norwegians and Danes in isolated areas can't understand the dialects in other parts of their own countries.) They share a common state religion, traditions, customs, folklore, foods and more.

But a cultural unity in no way implies a political unity. For around the year 1000, when Leif the Lucky was first sighting North American shores, Denmark, Sweden and Norway had for several centuries been separate (but not necessarily unified) entities.

And the thousand years that have followed the Vikings' two centuries of dubious glory are a melange of rulers crowned and unseated, borders shifted and reestablished, stability and chaos, courage and cunning. There have been wars, alliances, counter-alliances, treaties, treaty abrogations, invasions, intrigue, murders, insurrections, abdications and constantly shifting power struggles between kings and nobles, between nobles and peasants and between peasants and kings — all until relatively recent centuries.

So in no way would we attempt to condense Scandinavian history into one chapter. Instead, we'd urge you to find a good general history of Scandinavia and read it as you would a historical novel. T. K. Derry's "A History of Scandinavia," published by University of Minnesota Press in

Scandinavians have a saying about their countries: "The land divides us; the sea unites us."

association with the American-Scandinavian Foundation, is a good one. An excellent feature of this book is a "Parallel Table of Events," showing what was happening in each nation at specific times and also in Scandinavian culture as a whole.

Or choose a leader or person in Scandinavian history and explore his or her career, learning to know that period of history as you do. You might choose Cnut the Great, whom the saga writer called "a man of great luck in anything connected with power." Or King Olav, who was sainted. Or Birgitta, who gave counsel to the Pope and had a religious influence on all of Europe. Or Christian IV, the restless Danish king who could not stop building soaring castles and Copenhagen's most beautiful buildings. Or Margaret, the skilful woman who was crowned the "Lady Queen" in Kalmar in 1397, climaxing her achievement of first uniting the three Scandinavian countries. Or Gustavus Adolphus, called by one of his officers "the Captain of Kings and the King of Captains." Or Grundtvig, the Danish preacher who urged a celebration of their common culture by all Scandinavians.

Living as we do in a land that was settled largely after these conflicts in Scandinavia had subsided, we find some things hard to understand. One thread, for instance, runs through the sweep of history that follows the Vikings: whether for good or ill, Christianity and the Church played a dominant role. The advent of Christianity to the North ended the pagan practices that included tossing non-perfect newborns out on the snow to die. But the Church as a powerful institution figured in countless bloody wars through succeeding centuries, wars that had little to do with the gospel of Christ but much to do with power and dominance.

Paganism gave way to Christianity almost without a whimper, although Viking chieftans held out for the old gods in many outlying areas. The Vikings may have been their own first missionaries. Some were converted on voyages to the south, others brought back stories of the new religion so that there was curiosity about it even before the first monks came north. As time passed, many of those who trafficked with traders from Christian Europe found it expedient for their business to embrace the new religion.

But the greatest change by far came when the current rulers themselves were converted to Christianity and invoked it on their nobles. Harald Bluetooth ("blue" has the old second meaning of "large") followed his father as a Danish king in 940. Having been baptized, Harald destroyed the pagan temple built by his father. This was no small feat, surrounded as Harald was by pagan officers. But Harald's son, Sven Forkbeard, started a rebellion in which Harald was killed, and reinstated the pagan customs. It fell to Cnut (Canute, Knute) to become the greatest influence in Chris-

In many Scandinavian areas you will find stones of unknown age set in circles. Called *dommaringar,* these "rings of judgment" are believed to be the prehistoric equivalent of our Senate and Supreme Court. Chiefs and notables of a clan would gather to hold trials and conduct the clan's business.

tianizing Denmark. Cnut forbade his earls to engage in pagan practices. He financed missionaries from England, and by the time he died other missionaries were moving from the south into Sweden.

In Norway, King Olaf had been baptized in Normandy and in 1024 set up a system of church law in Norway. Sweden was slower to embrace Christianity and it was not until the end of that century that the great pagan temple at Upsala was destroyed. But by the mid-1100s the Swedes were ready to launch a missionary effort in Finland. In Sweden as elsewhere, the monarchy came to be strengthened through its connection with the church.

If the transition from paganism to Christianity was relatively free of major bloodshed, the same cannot be said of the struggle between Catholicism and the Reformation. The last civil war in Denmark's history ended in 1536 with the establishment of Lutheranism. (The confiscation of Church lands helped King Christian III to meet his huge military expenses.) It also ended with the subjugation of Norway as a province of Denmark, a state that existed for almost 300 years.

And while the change came more gradually in Sweden, there followed civil war and an ensuing war in which Denmark sought and failed to reestablish the kingdom which included Sweden. Christian IV's disastrous efforts to add German lands to his own might have set the stage for a joint effort between Denmark and Sweden to counter forces friendly to Rome. Instead it was left to the Swedish King Gustavus Adolphus, the "Lion of the North," to lead victorious Protestant forces in the bitter and seemingly endless Thirty Years War in Europe.

It is interesting to note that in Scandinavia the Renaissance more or less followed the Reformation, rather than preceding it. For the first time the Bible was translated into the language of the people. The Norwegians sang hymns in their native Norwegian rather than the Danish that had been thrust upon them. The Danish heard their own language in the plays and writings of such men as Ludvig Holberg, rather than the German which was spoken in the Danish court. The Finns, who had never had a written language of their own, got one in order that the catechism might be taught. And the fact that reading was necessary to learning the catechism for confirmation led to minimal schooling even for the poor, though it was a long time in coming.

Pressured by high-ranking church leaders as well as by peasants who were becoming more and more enlightened and aware, rulers and the bureaucracy were forced to effect social changes. By the end of the 1700s slave trade had ended, relief for the poor had been improved and abuses in prisons began to be corrected. A system of conciliation courts was set up. Education of teachers was established. Humanitarian causes got even more attention in the early 1800s: public health, aid for the mentally ill, religious liberty and emancipation of women changed many cruel practices. It was not until 1814, however, that elementary education for ALL children was made mandatory in Denmark; in Sweden it was 1844 and in Norway 1860.

The Napoleonic Wars again divided the Scandinavians. The results were disastrous not only for Denmark, which had allowed itself to be pulled into an alliance with France, but for Norway, where the loss of their profitable exports brought terrible poverty, almost starvation. On the heels of this war came Sweden's war with Russia in which the loss of a key fortress led to Sweden's defeat and the surrender of Finland to Russia. It also brought about a new system of government in Sweden which limited the monarch's power but still guaranteed class privileges.

In 1814 an almost bankrupt Denmark agreed to surrender Norway to Sweden. But the Norwegians, dedicated to the sovereignty of the people and fired by the American and French Revolutions, drew up their own con-

Roskilde Domkirke,
Roskilde

stitution. And while they recognized Swedish King Charles XIII as King of Norway, they made it abundantly clear that he ruled only because the Norwegian people, acting through the Storthing, had elected him.

And in 1905, Norwegians forced negotiations on their demand for independence from Sweden. Pressed by other European leaders for a peaceful settlement of the question, Sweden agreed and a Danish prince was crowned King Haakon VII.

By the beginning of the 20th century, all three countries had moved into an industrialized era. New inventions and technical advances brought change but prosperity for Scandinavia was still tied to the prosperity of the rest of Europe. More liberal ideas and political parties that espoused them were on the upsurge and social change continued. It was expressed in child labor laws, old age pensions, housing standards and health insurance.

It also found expression in opposition to general conscription, a tenet that may have strengthened the resolve of the three countries to remain neutral in World War I. (It was at this time that both Finland and Iceland declared their independence.) Two decades later Sweden, although it mobilized 400,000 troops, managed to stay neutral during World War II. The Danes and Norwegians had no such choice. The Danish king and government surrendered when the bombing of Copenhagen was imminent. And while much has been written about Norway's courageous underground resistance to the Nazis during the German occupation, many are unaware that, earlier, heavy fighting took place along the Norwegian coast, especially at Trondheim and Narvik.

An Australian writer once said that "the Scandinavians are closer to having Civilization that deserves to be spelled with a capital C than any other countries in the world." Whether that Civilization will survive the stifling bureaucratic network and burgeoning social welfare costs that cloud Scandinavian horizons today remains to be seen. But if out of a pagan, war-torn, class-conscious past can come a people fiercely dedicated to human rights and a high quality of life for every citizen, something must have provided an impetus.

The Christian gospel? How can one say that when church attendance and participation are so notoriously low in Scandinavia? And yet, structured as it may be, given lip service only, often choked by cynical and self-righteous leaders, tied to wars, money, power struggles and bloody misdeeds, the Church and the Word have been part and parcel of Scandinavian life since the first monks plunged into the forest. And buried as it may be by other credos, other emphases, isn't it possible its kernel may have sent out roots that find expression in action?

It puts me in mind of a Japanese friend who commented that while Christians make up only one-half of one percent of Japan's population, all humanitarian changes have come as a result of the influence of that small percentage.

With the Scandinavians, it may be that the music isn't heard as it once was but they're singing the words.

3.

Folk Tales, Folk Lore

The best history is the kind that begins, "Once upon a time....." Scandinavia is full of this kind!

Here again much of the folk literature is based on the conflict between good and evil, between God and the Devil, between the Black Book of Magic and the Sign of the Cross.

But the tales go back far beyond the beginnings of the Christian era, beyond the Vikings, back to a dim past when man saw almost everything around him inhabited by spirits. And for those who eked a precarious livelihood from the stony fields and the sea, the most important thing in the world was to be on good terms with those spirits.

There is a fine line between folk tales and legends. A folk tale is pure fiction; none of the tellers meant it to be anything more. A legend started as an account of something that actually happened. But as the event was recounted around countless campfires, passed on to new generations, signed and colored with the teller's own imagination, it is hard to say where fact ends and fiction begins.

(This is not true of the Icelandic *sagas*. The word *saga* can be translated literally as "saying what it was." These grew from generations of men who were considered professionals in their craft of story telling. They memorized the tales that were recited to them and passed them on almost word for word. And in a land that had little intercourse with others, those heroic tales are the closest thing we have to early *factual* history.)

There is a root of similarity in the folk tales of every country. And in the Scandinavian lands, separated as their people have been from their neighbors by craggy mountains, deep fjords, impenetrable forests and ice-locked winters, the same legends and stories have been told for centuries in hundreds of separated valleys — but with local variations.

So prevalent are these tales in their many forms that students of folklore have actually catalogued them with their variations.

Here is an example:

The basic story is this: A minister was driving his cart with someone in it when the horse stopped abruptly. The wheel then dropped off. The minister ordered the devil, who had caused the mishap, to be off. Then he drove on. The next day it was observed that the wheel was no longer missing.

But in eastern Norway the story has been told for generations with these variations: They were driving at full speed, they drove into a duckpond; the boy who was driving the cart was told not to feed the horse and when he did the horse died; the minister was coming home from the house of a dying parishioner when it happened; the wheel was rolling beside the cart.

In Telemark these variations were found: the minister ordered the devil to carry the cart; sparks were flying; the devil whimpered and howled. A version from southern Norway has it that the cart was being driven over ice that was only one night old. A western Norway version says there was some dialogue with the devil over who was to pay for the cart.

Who knows what mishap sparked this story and how it came to be told in so many ways in so many isolated areas?

About 2,500 types of folk tales, stories that are current in Norwegian oral tradition, have been recorded. They are catalogued in manuscripts and catalogs of the *Norsk Folkeminnesamling*, the Norwegian Folklore Institute of Norway. Finnish scholar Antti Aarne was the first to devise a system of classifying such legends in international folklore. Radar Th. Christiansen sought to do the same with the "migratory legends," tales that are passed from one country to another and follow a definite pattern. He also calls these tales "memorates," accounts of actual experiences either by the teller or someone else, and almost always connected with some local landmark, area or person.

Strangely enough, in northern Norway, an area that is isolated and far from the rest of Scandinavia, the old stories that have been collected bear more resemblance to the tales of other countries than those of any other part of Norway or Sweden. This is likely because of the great seasonal fisheries here, when fishermen came from as far away as Finland and even northern Russia. While they waited out the storms, story-telling was their way of passing the time. And though their languages differed, stories managed to pass between them. Many of these were retold at home and a bit of embellishment added or a few changes made.

Here are two more examples of folk tales told differently in different areas:

The basic story: A woman familiar with witchcraft left home on an er-

~~~~~~

In the Middle Ages, the little island of Blåkulla (Blue Hill) in Kalmar Sound was believed by the Swedes to be the place where the witches gathered to receive their instructions from the Devil and to dedicate stolen children to him. Between 1668 and 1673 some vigorous witch hunts were carried out. Those who told of seeing witches or the Devil were allowed to go free if they would state that it was all their imagination. Surprisingly, most of them went to their deaths insisting it had all happened.

~~~~~~

rand. She told her maid to make butter but only to put three spoonsful of cream in the churn. The maid, however, put in seven. The cream flowed all over the kitchen. The witch, on her return, was angry.

In eastern Norway, the story goes that the cream flowed down into a neighboring valley where even now the cows will not touch the grass. Another version is that the cream overran the valley and now those are the best fields on the farm. The woman, it is reported elsewhere, had sold herself to the devil for "the black book and a green tweed skirt." (Scandinavian witches seemed to wear green, not black.) In Telemark, one account states that the witch was on her way to Hekkelfjell for the witches' sabbath. From Rogaland in western Norway comes the story that the witch, together with the girl, had gone to a wedding where they ran out of butter and the girl was sent home to make some.

Another story has this basic root: A man out at sea saw a sea-sprite or "marmennil," a tiny thing, standing on a fishhook. Out of pity the fisherman threw a mitten to the little creature to protect it from the cold. As a reward he caught plenty of fish. Later the same being appeared and in a rhymed message warned him of an approaching storm. The man made for the shore at once. His comrades made fun of him, but a terrible tempest arose and many fishermen were drowned.

Most accounts of this story have been collected along Norway's west and northern coast. Some add that it is good to throw "a mitten to the merman" for then he will tell how fishing will come out. In one account the merman complained of the cold so the fisherman threw him a mitten. Another says the fisherman gave the "marmal" a coat and tried to bring him ashore but the "marmal" insisted on being put back in the sea. And finally, some versions include the warning that if you catch a "marmal," you'd better give him a piece of clothing or he will take his revenge.

Generally these "once upon a time" stories of the past concern 1) the devil and the Black Book of Magic; 2) witches and witchcraft; 3) ghosts and the human soul; 4) spirits of rivers, lakes and the sea; 5) trolls and giants; 6) fairies; 7) domestic spirits such as the *nisse* in Norway and the *tomte* in Sweden; 8) local legends about places, events and persons, as, for instance, the account of how the site of a church was selected by supernatural signs.

A legend told among the Lapps and Finns as well as all Scandinavians is that of the Christmas midnight Mass of the Dead. Most common is the story of an old woman who passed by the church at midnight Christmas Eve and saw it all lighted up. "God help me, I must be late for the *julotta* (early morning service)!" she exclaimed and went in. She recognized several of the worshippers as former members of the congregation who had died. She was warned to jump over the threshold on her way out, but her coat caught on a nail in the doorway — and she was dead in a matter of weeks. Another version of the story has the sexton coming early to make the church ready for the *julotta* and finding the dead, some dressed in black and some in white. They were worshipping with the late pastor of the parish. Frightened, he climbed the stairs to the bell tower and crawled astride the bell, which pealed out.

One writer, Margaret Sperry ("Scandinavian Stories"), assesses Danish folk tales as being whimsical, humorous and full of common sense. Those of Finland are poignant and full of beautiful heartbreak. Icelandic eddas and sagas, she believes, are "too brutal" for the child mind, while in Lapland the long winter darkness can create in a child's mind "a dread of the forces of nature." Norway's tales are characterized by humor — sharp, even grotesque humor, while Sweden's portray peasant life with abiding faith that goodness will prevail in the end.

Originals of many Norwegian folk tales are found in a four-volume collection by the famous Norwegian folklorists Asbjörnsen and Moe, who compare favorably with the Brothers Grimm in Germany. They traveled extensively in the valleys and mountains of Norway and listened to tales from people who in turn had heard them from the lips of their elders.

Scandinavian legends are peopled with a motley assortment of other-worldly characters. There are of course the originals, the great Thor, driver of chariots across the sky, and Freya, goddess of all that made the seed break open and the fields yield green in the spring.

But there are also mountain-sized trolls with two heads and three eyes, who carried the spare eye in one hand and lured unsuspecting maidens into their troll kingdom inside the mountains. There are hulder, troll maidens

Some troll women have noses so big a smaller troll may set up housekeeping on one!

who are as beautiful as any human maiden until you note that they have tails. If a hulder marries a human in a church ceremony, the tail will drop off but they will always be gifted with a certain second sight that humans do not have. There are child trolls, meaner and uglier than their parents, and trolls who steal newborn infants and leave one of their own instead.

Trolls are BIG. Norwegian legends in which trolls figure are often connected with some landmark, such as isolated boulders or stones, steep valleys or striking formations of hills. All were at one time explained as being the work of either giants or trolls. Cliff formations are trolls turned to stone. Very popular are tales of trolls who threw stones at churches, and the stones — usually huge boulders — are still there although they missed the church.

If trolls needed inventing, it may have been the Pope's men who invented them. Churchmen sent by Rome to develop the newly-introduced Christianity to Norway and Sweden trained as priests many men who had only recently been converted from paganism. It was almost impossible to eliminate the pagan gods completely; it may have been easier to banish them to the impenetrable mountain heights where they and their progeny lived out the centuries.

In one tale the daughter of a troll, seeing a farmer plowing, seized him and his horse and carried them off in her apron. "Father, see my new plaything!" she called. But the troll father told her to carry them back and "set them down carefully." In another tale, a farmer is asked to ferry a troll across a river. But the farmer, alarmed at the size of the troll, asks him to alter his size. The troll refuses, but lops off a thumb from his mitten, fills it with gold and leaves it on the ferry for the farmer, to remind him of his size.

Stories of trolls and fairies usually bore a lesson. A certain fisherman did not observe the Sabbath but continued to work, even on holy days. One night he overheard two trolls: "May I borrow your cauldron?" "What are you going to use it for?" "To boil Lars." "Yes, you may borrow it if I may have the scrapings." "No, in that case I would rather roast him over the coals." Needless to say, Lars mended his ways and there was no more fishing on the Sabbath and holy days!

Many troll tales were straight-out moralizing: "Don't tell a lie or your nose will grow as long as a troll's and you can use it to stir the kettle!" Like many a Scandinavian, the late Arthur Stavig drew on "troll teaching stories" told him by his Norwegian grandfather, who left Norway for America in 1875. In his several books on trolls, Stavig names them : *fossegrimen,* the troll of music; *risse-gubben,* forest troll; *nokken,* water

The fearsome noek, or water troll.

troll; *brotrollet,* the bridge troll; *Dovre-gubben,* King of the Trolls, and more. The stories carried morals like "bad accidents tag the footsteps of careless people" and "there are some things one should never do even to save himself."

But there ARE trolls that are almost likable. Or are they elves? Or fairies? These are the little domestic spirits, generally called *nisse* in Norway and *tomte* in Sweden. In Norway they are also known as *haugetusse, tusse and gobonden.* They may be helpful or annoying and mischievous, depending on their mood or the lesson they hope to teach the residents of their farm or home. One may live in the barn, seeing to it that the cow gets enough hay even if it means stealing it from a neighbor. Or one may live under the eaves of a house, listening to the conversations inside, determining the fate of the crops on how agreeable or quarrelsome he finds his host family.

There is a special *jul nisse* or *jul tomte* or *julvätten,* as the poet Victor Rydberg of Sweden called him, though he is of a more recent origin (no doubt originating as a tiny Santa Claus). He's the one who brings gifts to the children and checks to make sure the farmer has been good to his cattle on Christmas Eve. It was as an illustration for one of Rydberg's stories about the *jul tomte* that Jenny Nystrom's drawings of *tomtes* first appeared. Before long her version of the tiny fellow with his long beard, red stocking cap and homespun clothing was the one and only *jul tomte* — and no one has been able to change him! And while serious art critics found it hard to accept Jenny as an artist rather than a craftsperson, she has in later years come into her own as one of Sweden's best loved artists.

There is less fear and more humor in stories about these domestic elves. One family was so grateful for all the help their house-nisse had given them that they put out a beautiful new outfit of clothes for him. The next day he announced that he was now dressed far too fine to do menial work — and he disappeared forever.

One farmer had a troublesome *nisse* who caused so much trouble it made the farmer's life unbearable. In desperation he packed all his belongings to leave the farm. When the chest was loaded on the wagon, a neighbor called, "Where are you going?" The lid of the chest popped open and the troublesome *nisse* piped, "We're moving today!"

There are folk tales of a later time that must be included here if for no other reason than to show the delightful humor of the Danes. They're like the Polish jokes that some people told until Poles objected. They're like the Norwegian jokes that Swedes still tell and the Swede jokes that Norwegians still tell.

As far back as the 1700s, the people of Mols in Denmark were for some reason singled out by their fellow Danes to be the butt of "yokel jokes." A printed collection of these stories came out in the 1770s, a second edition in 1780 and another in 1866. (The story of the lobsters first appeared in a collection published in Norway in 1871.) Here are four of the stories:

36

Three Molsboes were watching the sun set when it dawned on them that it always went down in the west. Then they recalled with equal astonishment that it always came up in the east. One declared that it must "go under us" at night; another said no, it "goes on north, so far that we cannot see it."

But the third one gave them a withering look. "Of course it goes back the same way it came, you fine fools. It's just that it's night and we cannot see it!"

An old man of Mols heard that a Norwegian ship had anchored at Ebeltoft. He had never seen a Norwegian so he decided to go down and greet them. But the crew had gone ashore for the day and the only living things the old man could find aboard were some lobsters that had escaped from a basket and were crawling about on deck.

He scratched his head in puzzlement. But since no one else was around, then this must be the crew. He put out his hand to one of them, saying, "Good day to you, little father," and got a stinging bite on the hand. He roared with pain but managed to get his hand free. None of the crew ventured a word, so the old man bade them goodbye but was smart enough not to extend his hand again.

"They're only a little people, those Norwegians," he told his neighbors when he got back. "Aye, they're little, but they're tough, with a good grip on things. You know that as soon as you shake hands."

There are two versions of this story: A Molsbo man, finding a slice of white bread on the road and (raised on black rye bread) never having seen such a thing before, finally picked up the courage to taste it. In one version he tells his friend, "If only I had bread like this I'd eat it." In another version he says, "I'd eat this if only I had some bread to eat it with."

A Molsbo, wearing his best clothes for a visit to town, took his homeward way after having done a little more than just quench his thirst. After a bit he sat down to rest on the road's edge and promptly fell asleep.

A poor craftsman on his way to town in search of work noticed the Molsbo's fine new stockings. He couldn't resist exchanging them for his own, which were dirty and full of holes.

Shortly after, there came a man driving a horse and wagon. "Pull in your legs," he shouted, "or I'll drive over them."

The Molsbo opened his eyes sleepily, looked down at his legs but did not see the spotless white stockings his mother had given him that morning. He did not move.

"Drive on, my friend," he called. "Those are not my legs!"

Is there a value to folklore? And if so, is it purely in the moral lesson it conveys? Maybe Sven Grundtvig, the Danish folklorist, summed it up best:

"The present should interpret the past, purely and clearly, so that the future will understand and be inspired by it."

Hans Christian Anderson

Though the Danes might prefer to be remembered for other persons, other accomplishments, there's no doubt that they love their famed storyteller as much as the rest of the world does.

From the Little Mermaid in Copenhagen's harbor to the Goose Girl in porcelain and the Beautiful Swan in glass, mementos and memories of Hans Christian Andersen abound in Denmark.

In Odense, crowds line up at the Hans Christian Andersen Museum to view pieces of his life — the huge house slippers that warmed his ungainly feet, the top hat that emphasized his overly large head, the coat with long sleeves that still never seemed to cover his bony wrists. And all over the world children who have never heard his name love him through the tales he told, tales retold to generation after generation.

Who knows how much those gentle tales owe to the old stories told by Hans Christian's mother and *Bestamor*, his grandmother? Theirs were tales of trolls and goblins and magical curses and signs in the sky. These Hans Christian's shoemaker father sought to counteract by reading to him the works of the great Danish playwright Holberg. Barely able to scratch together enough for food, the book-loving shoemaker was determined to open his son's mind to a world he could only know through books. In a one-room house scarcely big enough for the three of them, the shoemaker and his lanky, akward son spent the long evenings building puppet theaters, dressing puppets, putting on plays — and telling stories.

Born April 2, 1805, in Odense on the island of Fyn, Hans Christian Andersen knew abject poverty as a child and a youth. The poverty was even more painful because his dreams soared so high. He wanted to be a GREAT actor. He ached to be RECOGNIZED as a writer. He was determined to be Denmark's most FAMOUS novelist. He wanted to be accepted and loved, most of all for the works he would create both for the stage and the printed page.

To a degree he achieved the latter, perhaps more outside Denmark than in it. His exuberance and childlike innocence won him friends and supporters and in time no less a patron than the King of Denmark made it possible for Andersen to receive an education. He wrote furiously, turning out novels and plays that sometimes won mild acclaim, sometimes scorn.

When he was 30 and waiting for the publication of "The Improvisator," Andersen whiled away some time writing — and publishing — a small pamphlet of tales for children. A man who

Bestamor

had put him through his examinations at the University made a prophetic statement to Andersen at that time.

" 'The Improvisator' may make you famous, but the children's tales will make you immortal."

Andersen disagreed.

By the time he was 40, Andersen was a well-known literary figure. He wrote one novel after the other. He wrote plays that were presented at the Royal Theatre. And though he insisted the fairy tales were nothing but "trifles," he continued to write them. After all, he loved children and loved to entertain them, and the little books did bring in income. But there was this, too, that in their settings with elves and giants and fairy queens and humble peasants, Andersen could stick pins into some of the pompous society of that time. In "The Emperor's New Clothes," for instance, his own experiences with sham and pretense laid a cutting edge on every line.

Even without these reasons, Andersen may have had to write the stories. They were simply "there." Every cranny of his agile mind was packed with tales, large and small, that he had listened to from infancy. Mingled, crowded, mulled over, distilled, they were a teeming ground from which sprang characters shaped anew by Andersen's loving spirit.

That he put them on paper in his almost illegible scrawl is the whole world's gain. Hans Christian Andersen might have been remembered as an acceptable Danish novelist and playwright. But it is the fairy tales that truly did make this insecure and frustrated Dane immortal.

~~~~~~

Hans Christian Andersen's wit was irrepressible. Among the jottings in his notebook:

"A man had a beautiful beech tree. The young lady from the great farm nearby often said, upon seeing the tree, 'You must have it painted! It is lovely! It deserves to be painted.'

"On the young lady's birthday the man had the bark scraped off and the whole tree painted — red with yellow stars.

"The tree died."

~~~~~~

The Gods of Legend

While Hans Christian Andersen's stories are surely the best known and most loved of all Scandinavian stories, they are not typical of the historic Nordic folk tale. Andersen's stories are for the most part gentle and humorous. Even when they contain biting satire, it is cloaked in velvet.

But the old folk tales, told over campfires and by itinerant craftsmen, were tales of violence and mayhem.

One reason may have been the harsh northern climate. Life was a constant battle with the elements — the bitter cold, the long nights of winter, the storms that flogged the coastline, the sea that swallowed their small boats, hunger and cold — always the battle raged against hunger and cold.

Too, most of the tales had roots in the legends of the Norse gods. And in those pre-Christian beliefs, there was little that spoke of comfort and caring. The gods, it seemed, existed largely to inspire warriors to fight to the death. For it was then that these most daring and adventurous of them might be carried by the golden-helmeted Valkyries into Valhalla, where the walls were formed of spears and the roof plated with golden shields.

There was Odin, king of the gods, whose helmet was shaped like an eagle and who lived on mead alone so that his hunting hounds might have his food. There was Loki, god of fire, and Loki's child, the Midgard serpent, whose tail reached around the world and who churned the seas when he was angry.

There were Sol and Mani, gods of the Sun and the Moon, who drove their chariots across the sky pursued by two wolves who wanted to return the world to darkness. There was Heimdall, watchman of the gods, whose ears were so keen he could hear wool grow on the backs of sheep.

There was Thor, most feared of the gods, driving his chariot across the sky until sparks lit up the heavens and the wheels cracked and roared, echoing over the jagged mountain peaks.

There was Frigga (Freya), wife of Odin, at home in her castle in the mists, spinning golden thread and carrying at her side the keys to the great storehouse of the gods. And Baldur, the beautiful, most loved of all the gods. But even the good and beautiful did not escape danger, and Baldur died, his heart pierced by a sprig of mistletoe.

And always there was conflict — conflict between the gods and the giants at the beginning of time; between the Frost Giants and the Flame Giants; between the Norns (Fates) who guarded the tree of life and those who would steal its fruit; between evil and good; between power and cunning.

The Tomtes of Hellerup

Here is a charming example of a regional folk tale that concerns a particular place. It is translated and adapted from "Hallandska Herregårdar" by Peter von Muller, published 1871.

In the rolling hills of southern Sweden, in the province or *lan* of Halland, lies a lovely old farmhouse, a *herregård*. There is a story that has been told and retold through the generations about the tomtes who once lived behind the rain barrel in the kitchen of Hellerup.

There was once a young woman, as good and kind as she was beautiful, who lived at Hellerup. One night she woke to a sudden small sound beside her bed. She was terrified to see in the pale moonlight beside her bed a *tomtegubbe* (elf man), dressed in the familiar gray outfit and wearing the well known red tasseled stocking cap.

"Don't be afraid, kind mistress," whispered the strange little figure. "I don't want to harm you. I only wish to ask a favor. And you who are so good and kind to everyone surely will not deny me this request.

"For a long time now my people and I have lived in your kitchen, in the corner where the big water barrel stands. But the barrel is old now and beginning to crack. It leaks. And the maids are careless and spill water around it, so we cannot even stay dry while we sleep. We are plagued by dripping and dampness, and I'm sure you agree this is no healthy state. So — would you be so kind as to have the barrel moved?"

"Of course," whispered the young woman. And true to her word, the very next morning she called in two of the hired hands and had the barrel moved to another corner of the kitchen.

(Through all the years that followed in Hellerup, the barrel was occasionally moved back to its original corner. But each time, even though it might not be leaking, everything seemed to go wrong in the kitchen. So there was nothing to do but to move it away from the *tomtes'* corner again. Then the *tomtes* returned, hanging up the fallen pots, causing the bread to rise as it should, even keeping the porridge from burning to the bottom of the pot.)

Not long after the first visit from the strange little elf-man, the young woman had a second visit. This time he invited her to a christening.

"But come at once," he whispered. "We are ready and waiting for you." There was no time to bring out her "Sunday dress" so she quickly slipped into her everyday dress and apron, which was

42

all laid out for the morning.

And though the old farmhouse was neither enormous nor a labyrinth of passageways, she would never be able to describe the route they followed that night, though she knew that at one point it led through the kitchen.

Surprise of surprises, she was to be the godmother of the adorable little *tomte* baby! After the child was properly doused with water, the young woman handed the tiny girl child back to its mother. "Hold out your apron," commanded the mother and dropped something into it. Though it appeared to be only small wood shavings, the girl showed sincere appreciation for this unusual gift. Then she was led again by a strange, unfamiliar route until she found herself in the great hall on the main floor. Here the *tomte* drew her aside.

"We will no doubt meet again," he nodded, his eyes darting about the room just beginning to be lit by the dawn. "But, remember, whatever you may see, never laugh at me or mine, for then we shall never see each other again."

After the little man bade her goodbye, the young woman dropped the wood shavings into the fireplace, thinking they might be of use in starting the fire in the morning. But when the maid came to light the fire, there lay a mass of glowing gold ornaments, hammered as if by a tiny forge and inlaid with shining black enamel.

(The jewels were handed down through several generations but in later years seem to have disappeared as mysteriously as they came.)

Time went by. On a glorious June day, near the midsummer, wearing the jewelled gifts, the young woman stood as a bride in that same great hall.

But the guests whispered among themselves.

"Why does she look as if her thoughts were miles away?" and "Why does she keep looking away?"

For the bride's eyes were riveted on the huge stove in the corner of the hall. There, out of sight of the guests, were her tiny friends assembled for a wedding of their own. And the little bride was none other than her own god-daughter!

Everything proceeded in exactly the same way that the ceremony in the room was being carried out. There was food and drink at tiny tables, just as the tables in the great hall were overflowing.

But suddenly one of the *tomte* servers, who was passing a tray of tiny *berlinerkranser*, tripped on a splinter and fell flat on his face. The daughter of the household forgot the warning of the *tomte* and exploded into laughter.

In the blink of an eye the scene vanished. And the *tomtes* have never been seen at Hellerup since.

Legend of the
Christmas Rose

Not so well known as some of the Christmas stories and legends is that of the Christmas rose. But you will find the flower in Scandinavian needlework, often in exquisite cross stitch. The Christmas rose is white.

There are many versions of the legend. Selma Lagerlof wrote a beautiful account of it. You may find it in anthologies of Christmas stories (Robert Lohan's "Christmas Tales for Reading Aloud," for one) or in the Lagerlof book, "The Legend of the Christmas Rose."

In a long ago time, Sweden banished its outlaws to a primitive forest region where they lived out their sentence, often with wife and children. One of these wives boasted to the local abbot how every year at Christmas Goinge forest was transformed into a beautiful garden to commemorate the hour of Christ's birth. She was finally persuaded to lead the abbot, together with a lay brother, into the deep and craggy wilderness.

As they waited that night of Christmas Eve in the robber's cave, a strange illumination began to spread over the forest. The trees budded, the birds began to sing, flowers burst into bloom and berries formed on bushes, the fox and rabbit paraded their young.

The abbot was in a state of delight, trying to find the loveliest flower to bring to his archbishop. For the archbishop had promised pardon for the robber family if the abbot could produce just one flower from the promised spectacle.

But suddenly the lay brother could contain himself no longer. Surely all this, revealed as it was to these evil-doers, must not be of God but of the Devil. When a dove lighted on his shoulder he shouted, "Go thou back to hell from whence thou came!"

In an instant the scene began to fade and slowly it disappeared. And the abbot lay dead on the snow. Clutched in his hand was a pair of white root bulbs, nothing more.

The lay brother planted them in the cloister but nothing came up and they were forgotten. But when Christmas Eve came round, green leaves pushed through the snow, crowned by silvery white petals. Overcome with awe, the brother took the flowers to the archbishop. True to his promise, he pardoned the robber.

Goinge forest never bloomed again. But the Christmas rose remains as a memory and a reminder that even to the least deserving of all the Christ reveals himself.

Once when I had baked rosettes at Christmas time, an elderly Norwegian lady chided me gently for dipping them in granulated sugar.

"They should have just a dusting of powdered sugar over them," she told me. "It is the snow on the Christmas rose."

4.

The Home Arts

Scandinavians love their homes.

Remember Grandma's kitchen on a Saturday afternoon? Scrubbed, starched and shining, it was heady with the cardamom-cinnamon fragrance of the day's baking ("yust in case someone should come"). Over the oilcloth-covered table lay a cross-stitched lunch cloth starched and ironed to a paper-like sheen. It had no creases; just as they did in the "fest rooms" of ancient Sweden, so Grandma rolled her starched and ironed linens on paper cylinders and stored them in a long drawer. In the center of the table zinnias and cosmos stood stiff-necked in a carnival glass bowl. And under the bowl was Great Grandma's wooden plate with the painted words, long weathered, *"I Jesu nam gå vi till bord."*

A far cry back, wasn't it, to the post-Viking house of logs, sod and stone; low, one-roomed, windowless, sooty, with dirt floor or rough planking, smelling of smoke and salt fish and wet wool?

And yet from these origins came the home arts that flowered in Scandinavia from earliest times until the industrial revolution. Fading for a time, they are now being joyously and enthusiastically revived.

Looking at the Vikings, we saw that as farming increased, houses came to be rectangular and fairly large (often as long as 90 feet), with a shed for the cattle at one end. Moving the cooking fire inside made it more comfortable, but from the fire pit in the middle of the room a constant veil of eye-stinging, wall-blackening smoke swirled its way to the single hole in the ceiling.

~~~~~~

The main room of a 1600s farmhouse was a large one in-which cooking, eating and sleeping all took place. But a cross beam by the fireplace indicated the kitchen boundary and another cross beam in front of the table indicated a "space of distinction." A stranger, possibly a beggar, would have to wait by the "beggar's beam" — the kitchen boundary — until the head of the house gave him permission to come further.

~~~~~~

But even while the homes were anything but pleasant, there was no lack of artistry in the people. Consider the grace of the Viking ships, the jewelry found in old Viking caches, even the centuries-old tapestries brought up from icy waters. The love and appreciation of beauty was there, but for the common man and his family, expression of it in the home came slowly.

Two developments, more than any others, helped to change this, giving impetus to what we think of as home crafts or folk arts in those countries.

The first was the coming of Christianity, first to Denmark, then to Norway and lastly to Sweden. It forced a sometimes reluctant North to become part of Europe and brought churches and church art to the people. Because the later Reformers ruthlessly destroyed every vestige of this early church decoration, we can only guess at the carved saints and cherubs and madonnas that graced the new church walls. Carpenters, wood carvers, metalsmiths and painters came from the continent, bringing their crafts and ready to be imitated. This the Scandinavians did, but with their own interpretations. The old and the new were melded together.

As Janice S. Stewart puts it in her excellent book, "The Folk Arts of Norway," the old civilizations were not displaced but "absorbed much of what Europe had to offer and applied it to the local situation."

Lending almost as great an impetus to home arts was the introduction in the 17th century of the masonry fireplace with chimney. These were usually built in a corner of the room. Gone was the fire pit, gone was the soot and smoke. Windows came into being. Now the bare walls could be hung with tapestries on festive occasions. Cupboards and chairs could be painted. White goods could be embroidered — and exposed.

The Renaissance reached Sweden late in the 16th century and Norway early in the 17th, but it had little effect on furniture decoration, weaving patterns or embroidered hangings until late in the 17th century. In many places it brought no changes at all.

For an interesting thing was happening in both Norway and Sweden. While peasant art was at first influenced by the art of the nobility, each individual valley and small isolated region was developing a style very much its own.

In fact, says Iona Plath, author of another outstanding book on this subject, "The Decorative Arts of Sweden," Swedish peasant art forms are not so much typical of Sweden as they are "typical of the individual province from which they originated." If anything, this was even more true of Norway.

For this reason, some authorities believe that a more descriptive term for this art of the common people would be "provincial art."

By the mid-1800s, industrialization was taking its toll. It was not only that poorer folk, like the more privileged, wanted "bought" goods. Circumstances actually forced them to buy.

For as industry forced out home producers, families had to move to cities where they could make a living in factories. Homes there were smaller, there was neither room nor time for a loom. Almost overnight the working and producing class became the great consumer class, having to buy goods that were often shoddy.

Fortunately, Scandinavians recognized what was being lost. Organizations like the National League of Swedish Home Craft Associations and Swedish Homecraft Association, Norwegian Home Arts Association and Danish Handcraft Guild stepped in. Not only do they protect and encourage home industries, but they constantly strive to improve the tastes and standards of the buying public.

Because of this, we have the best of this art available. Not only are there delightful examples of ancient folk art in museums and private collections, as well as books on the subject. But we also have a constant parade of new designs from Scandinavia, many of them (like the eight-pointed star in weaving, needlework and woodcarving) going back hundreds of years for their inspiration.

Let's look at those crafts most often done at home— crafts that you and I might learn and carry on fairly easily.

Woodcarving

Home styles varied from area to area, but a fairly typical peasant home had two rooms separated by a hall. In the main room the family ate, slept, cooked, baked and carried on their daily chores. Here the mother spun, wove, knit and sewed. The father had a work table by a window. Here he might in his free time make items for the home, or he might carry on a trade that served others living on the big *gård* — tailoring, clock-making, wood-carving, shoemaking, tinsmithing, painting. A woodworker clear up to the beginning of the 20th century might make in his home barrel staves and hoops, rakes, spade handles, wooden spoons and other items, all taken to market days and sold.

Across the hall (in which winter coats and boots were shed) was the "chest room" or storage room. Depending on the family's circumstances,

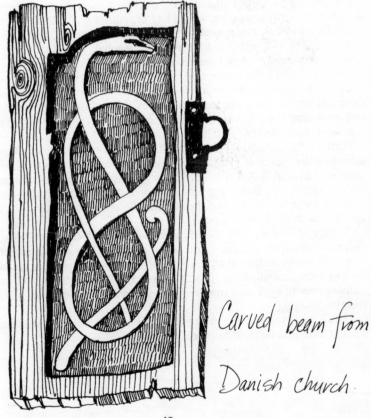

Carved beam from Danish church.

any number of chests were lined around the wall to hold their "church clothes." Others held linens and wall hangings that were brought out only for weddings, christenings and Christmas. The chest room also became the "fest room" for those special occasions, when it was hung with all the tapestries and embroidered linens the family had managed to store away in the chests.

The chests were likely made by the man of the house as were the rough benches (in earlier times made into beds at night), stools, shelves and chairs. Tables and built-in beds that lined the walls almost like cupboards were probably built by a carpenter. (Tables were unknown in ancient times; one tucked a bowl in one's lap or held it on a "lap board.") Three-legged chairs were popular. With the Renaissance, low cupboards became popular with the nobility and soon the peasant farmers adopted — and adapted — these, too.

Woodcarving was an ancient art, but with growing emphasis on home decoration it flourished anew. They carved on furniture, chests, door panels, candleholders, ale bowls, flour boxes, butter molds, plates, pudding dishes, food boxes. The latter, with their ingenious lids and handles (now often seen with *rosemaling*), carried food to gatherings at other farms and later became the lunch box for working men. The pudding or porridge bowls were used to carry a thick barley gruel to the neighbor woman who had just given birth.

Chip carving made use of geometric patterns with roots in pagan times. Scratch carving was light and airy. Wood burning was sometimes combined with carving. The acanthus vine, seen in so much church decoration, was part of the striking baroque scrolled work found especially in Norway's Gudbrandsdal area

And while some articles were embellished by carvers who made their living at the craft, there was one item the young Norwegian must make himself — the mangle tree. This was a flat board with a carved top and handle, used with a wooden roller for ironing, and was a traditional engagement present. (The story is told that one man had half a dozen mangle trees — each time a young woman changed her mind and returned his board he began carving a new one for his next choice!)

Painting

The term "decorative painting" covers the *blomstermålning* of Sweden and the more familiar *rosemaling* of Norway. Both are literally translated "flower painting." And while they are closely related to the folk painting of Russia and the Pennsylvania Dutch, they have their own distinctions. Perhaps more than any other folk art, they are closely identified with the local areas where they were done.

Just as some of the earlier carving art received impetus from the coming of Christianity to the North, so this later painted art was influenced by the Reformation. As Luther's religion supplanted Catholicism, handsome old churches were retained but all traces of so-called "popery" had to be wiped out. As an example, it's recorded that around 1600 all the churches in Norway's Gudbrandsdal district received new decorations. Imagine the wealth of artists, most of them again from the continent, who painted the length and breadth of the three lands. The somber saints were replaced by Biblical scenes, swirling and trailing acanthus vines and leaves, ribbons and banners and flowers.

Again, local artists watched, copied and adapted.

The use of these painted designs in homes began early in the 1700s. From then until roughly 1875, professional painters traveled through Sweden and Norway painting walls, furniture and all kinds of household articles.

Broadly speaking, Swedish and Norwegian decorative painting are quite different.

In southern Sweden, painted hangings began to be used alongside the long-favored tapestry hangings. For special occasions when neighbors and relatives might gather, any open wall space was covered either with tapestries or painted scenes. Large scenes, painted on linen or heavy paper, were attached to the exposed ridgepole and then to the side walls. As Plath says in her book mentioned earlier, "If the room resembled the inside of a tent, so much the better."

In northern Sweden, and especially in Dalarna, much of the painting was done directly on the wall. Sometimes there are long, horizontal panels that run the whole length of the wall. As many as 80 painters were active in Dalarna. They filled the spaces with architectural backgrounds, people and "kurbits," great, proliferate floral sprays, referring in name to the "kurbit" *(cucurbita)* which the Lord caused to grow up and shade Jonah in Ninevah.

Most of all, it's the depiction of people that make much of Swedish folk painting different from the Norwegian. Only in the eastern regions that adjoin Sweden did Norwegian painters put humans in their art.

The Swedish characters are usually from the Bible, but depicted in the dress of the time in which they were painted. Joseph and his brothers are shown as Swedish burgers. There is the Last Supper with all the disciples in

Swedish military uniforms. Others are ordinary people doing ordinary things — trading horses, traveling, going to a tavern, fighting. Many are on horseback or in carriages. There is humor in many of them. Some painters specialized in humorous paintings, and would include humorous sayings above or below the painting, even conversations.

There is less shading than in Norwegian *rosemaling*. The style is more flat, but sometimes color laid over color gives the effect of shading. Elaborate borders surround the main design.

Much of Norway's *rosemaling* can be identified as coming from a particular district. Many present day *rosemalers* are described as painting "in the Telemark style" or "in the Hallingdal tradition," so distinctive were the ways in which local artists painted.

But the game of identifying them is made more difficult by the fact that those early-day painters were itinerant. Some were farmers who painted in

Two or three hundred years ago, the traveling artist would be invited to spend a night or two at a farm as he passed through. When he left he might carve a little horse or two for the children. Today the red Dala horse with its colorful trim has become almost a symbol for Sweden, at least in this country. It's a cottage industry that grew into a huge operation, still under the ownership of the original family.

winter and took time from their farming in summer to travel to other districts to sell their wares. More commonly a full-time painter would stay at a farm long enough to complete several paintings, then move on to another and eventually to a different valley. Painters in that valley would absorb ideas from his work and combine them with their own. Comparing and imitating those styles is one of the things that makes *rosemaling* classes so fascinating today!

Norwegian folk painting decorated objects in the home as much or more than it produced wall paintings. Designs like stylized wide-petal flowers, buds, leaves and tear-drop accents are well suited to smaller projects. Hallingdal painters loved roses and vital colors. They held detail to a minimum.

Telemark painters were known for their swirling vines and leaves and highly decorative root-stem-leaf-flower unit. Gudbrandsdal, a main passage between east and west, had more continental influence. Green, blue and red-brown backgrounds were favorites. There are all kinds of rich, colorful, exciting variations.

Norwegian teachers of *rosemaling* come to America today to hold classes and workshops. There are also many excellent American teachers of the art. One of their main concerns, as is true of folk costume enthusiasts, is to keep the art authentic, as close as possible to what it was in the era when it flowered.

But here also lies a danger.

In 1979 Anund Lunden of Grungedal, Norway, known as one of the "grand old men" of *rosemaling*, was a guest of the Norwegian-American Museum in Decorah, Iowa, and taught two sessions of classes there. Lunden, often a judge at Norway's largest *rosemaling* exhibit, held at the Handelsstevne in Skien, was asked about the state of the art.

"No new directions," Lunden replied. "This is something which concerns me with the *rosemaling* I have seen in Skien and elsewhere. Everything is so much alike, repetition on repetition with only little variations. They could use more freedom, more imagination, and other forms."

He added that Sigmund Aarseth ("a phenomenon") has done "something new and it is good." He also noted that there is greater diversity of styles by painters in America than in Norway.

Weaving

In the far past, when men's and women's spheres were sharply defined, the fiber crafts were almost entirely women's work.

And an important one it was!

It was the *husfru* who kept the whole family in clothing and the house in bed coverings — these were the essentials. Beyond that she was expected to transform raw flax and wool into all the niceties that would give her household good standing: fine linen hangings to cover the walls and even the ceiling on special occasions, table covers, towels that were strictly ornamental, wool-nap robes to replace the fur robes in fishing boats.

Your great, great-grandmother probably began at the age of 12 to weave the linen cloth from which she would make the traditional embroidered wedding shirt for the man she would marry. (The reason so many of these shirts have come down to us in such good condition is that most girls made the shirt before they had any idea whom they would marry. Consequently, in spite of the loose fit and wide seams, the shirts almost never fit and were packed away without ever being worn out.) And no sooner was the proper young woman married than she would begin to spin, weave, sew and embroider the shirt in which her husband would eventually be buried.

Weaving room

To be sure, on the bigger farms the *husfru* had help. But here she was also expected to provide clothing for the hired help; an outfit of clothing was usually part of the pay. And while daughters began helping at an early age, it was a time-consuming task to train them in all the crafts. Grandmothers, aunts and elderly servant women who lived out their lives on the *gård* found their niche here. Many spinning wheels might whirr in one room against the clap-bang of the loom. Spinning was a social craft, and often farm women would carry their wheels to the next farm, spending a whole day spinning and catching up on the news.

From the time the flax was threshed and the wool left the sheep's back, the women of the house took over. Flax straw had to be dried over winter, soaked to rot the remaining husks, dried again, scraped, carded (combed) to straighten the fibers, and spun. Before the advent of spinning wheels the flax was spun by hand. The distaff used for this, as well as the scutching knife used for scraping and the batlet used to pound the finished linen in bleaching — all these were items the Danish or Norwegian suitor might elaborately carve for his true love. (The Swede, on the other hand, usually went to town and commissioned someone to knit his promised lady a pair of patterned mittens.)

Wool had less processes to go through, but it was a smelly business. Dying was sometimes done in an open shed that had an open hearth for baking or corn drying. Here yarns were boiled in homemade dyes of many kinds, including fermented urine, which produced a beautiful blue shade.

Although Sweden is best known for beautiful weaving, the history of the craft varies little between the three countries. New ideas, like the Flemish picture weaving of the Renaissance, reached Denmark first, Sweden and Norway soon after. But common to each are designs that go back to the 13th century and methods that began in Viking times.

For weaving was and is more than a utilitarian craft. It is an art form, and the beauty of Scandinavian weaving, I feel, lies in its servicability, the pleasure of its patterns and colors and its often traditional ties to a historic past.

A popular type of tapestry weave is *aklae* weaving, in which small squares form a large geometric design. It is used for wall hangings, rugs, bed coverlets, bench and pillow covers and is completely reversible. Swedish tapestries were often lighter in weight, using more harnesses on a loom and more linen thread. Sprang weaving made a lacy effect, like coarse lace. As far back as the sixth century braid was woven both for practical purposes and for trimming clothing. The finest linen weaving was used for caps and kerchiefs. Types of weaving, methods and pattern combinations are almost endless.

Scandinavian and Finnish *rya* rugs are very popular today. With their long wool nap, they were originally woven to replace animal furs as bed covers and sleigh robes. They were soft, thick and warm, but unlike the skins they did not get stiff and hard. They could be laundered and withstood salt water better, making them an asset in fishing boats.

Rogaland Rosemaling

© Trudy Sondrol Wasson 1983

This symmetrical design for Norwegian rosemaling came from the Hallingdal area along with the tulip and bonnet lily designs. The asymmetrical designs of old Rogaland rosemaling were done by painters influenced by Telemark painters. Typical background colors are black-green, dark blue, Norwegian blue (medium blue with a gray-green cast), teal blue and red. (Design is from "Old Rogaland Rosemaling" by Trudy Sóndrol Wasson, reprinted by permission.)

The Norwegian Lady

This is part of a counted cross stitch pattern of the famous *"Norwegian Lady"* statue in Virginia Beach, Virginia. Two identical statues, one in Virginia Beach and one in Moss, Norway, pay tribute to a Norwegian captain's wife, their small son and four seamen who lost their lives in a violent storm off Virginia in 1891. Design is by Tidewater Originals.

To get an idea of the use of these beautifully woven materials, try to imagine a wedding in very early times on a farm deep in a rural valley.

First and most important were the "church clothes." The bride would already have woven the bridegroom's shirt. All the rest of the family was outfitted. Now the house had to be made ready for the feasting that followed.

And feast time it was! The history of Ljungby parish in southern Sweden relates that a wedding went something like this: Guests gathered at the bride's parents' home in the morning and there were "several meals" during the day. Vows were spoken in the afternoon, and in the evening came feasting and dancing. Then the bridal pair left for their new home, but the next day they must hold *välkomstkalas* (welcome feast) with more food, music, dancing and games. But, the account adds, "further back in time the wedding feasting lasted several days. The record, when it comes to celebrating weddings in Ljungy parish, was nine days — three in the bride's home, three in the bridegroom's and three in the home to which the newlyweds moved!"

Getting the house ready meant covering walls and often ceiling with all the tapestries the house could muster. If the family could afford nothing better, then woven linen sheets were hung, some borrowed from neighbors. But in wealthier homes there would be *dukagang*, tapestries of white linen with blue wool yarn inserted to form a pattern which might be geometric, floral, or of animals, people and ships. If beds were exposed, they must have double-woven spreads and coverlets over the homespun straw ticking or striped linen feather tick. After the mid-1500s many of the woven hangings imitated those of the Flemish weavers, though the figures were more flat and direct. These had woven in them forms of lions, reindeer, elephants, unicorns and the strange dragon-like mythical beast, the *basilisk*.

Add to this the fine linen weaving on the feast table and the later painted panels suspended among the weavings, and you see what it meant to prepare for an "occasion."

Embroidery

For many of the home's textiles, weaving was only the beginning. Embroidery as an art form has flourished in Scandinavia through the centuries. Today it is routinely taught in the schools and there are also schools of embroidery.

Here it is safe to say that Denmark is the gateway through which many of these skills passed to Sweden and Norway, although many of these patterns and stitches, too, go back to crafts the Vikings likely brought back from their journeys.

Edith Nielsen, in her outstanding book, "Scandinavian Embroidery," comments that "no new stitches have been developed anywhere in the world since the 16th century." The way in which these stitches were used in many isolated Scandinavian areas have given them their distinctive character.

In an advertisement in a Danish newspaper in 1760, Carl John Netterberg announced that he was prepared to teach, in the student's home, such arts of embroidery as "couching, or raised work on muslin or silk, likewise cambric and linen, in the latter case also cut-work."

And in 1762 in the same newspaper was announced a sewing school where "daughters of gentlefolk may receive instruction in all forms of sewing and embroidery, such as samplers, toile de mousseline, various forms of white embroidery, also the making of flowers, the threading of pearls, the plaiting of hair bracelets with names and birds in them....."

In Denmark's fascinating Open Air Museum *(Frilandsmuseet)* is a "Lace School" that has been moved there from North Schleswig. It is a red brick house with a main dwelling area, a smaller dwelling area for a retired per-

~~~~~~

The Danish Handcraft Guild *(Haandarbejdets Fremme)* has incorporated into itself several associatons with their collections. These include the institute *"Vaevestuen,"* founded in 1913; *Hedebosyningens Fremme,* founded in 1908; The Society for the Benefit of Women's Needlework, founded in 1904, and The Society for Danish Arts and Handicrafts," founded in 1928. In addition, it founded in 1928 a school and a teachers' college which are now independent, state-accredited institutions. The teachers' college offers two majors, embroidery and clothing construction; the school offers five or ten-month courses in "Sewing for the Home."

~~~~~~

son and a cowshed at one end for a pig and a cow. Behind the kitchen of the main dwelling area is a room where, in the 1800s, the housewife taught lace-making to young girls. Each had a lace pillow on which she did her work, facing the windows to make use of the light. In the evenings they used a glass bulb filled with water to concentrate the light from a candle. Lace-making was an important industry around Tonder in western Schleswig, especially as a cottage industry in poorer homes.

The "toile de mousseline" mentioned in the sewing school advertisement became popular in Denmark in the 1800s and was variously known as "pulled thread work" and "drawn fabric embroidery." Done only on loosely-woven muslin, it had a soft, curving, floral-motif look, as opposed to the *hardangersom* of Norway, a more structured, geometric clipped-thread embroidery.

This embroidery, which originated in the Hardanger area of Norway (but is similar to work which Spanish peoples do), is enjoying a great revival in the United States today. Although many are learning it from books, others have been fortunate enough to find an *ekte Norsk* lady to teach them.

Mrs. Charles Quinn of Wells, Minnesota, learned the art from an elderly woman she visited in a nursing home. Mrs. Quinn went on to teach it to others and to publish several books on it. Corinne Otakie of Seattle went to her friend, Anna Hought, now 96, for instruction and has since taught many classes. Anna smiles as she remembers her first piece of hardanger work, a square tablecloth she made for her mother when she was 15. And

It's a little puzzling to hear that Swedish blouses are emboidered with *"prästakraga"* (preacher's collar). Actually, this is the common name for the marguerite, a small white flower.

two women in Fargo, North Dakota, Susan L. Meier and Rosalyn K. Watnemo, have built their interest in hardanger work into a thriving business handling supplies and pattern books.

Susan credits Mrs. A. E. (Marie) Hanson's efforts for the revival of interest in this emboidery in the Fargo-Moorhead area. But Mrs. Hanson's interest goes back to none other than a St. Olaf College president and his wife.

"Marie was first exposed to hardanger when her older sister was a student at St. Olaf College around 1902-1903," Susan explained. Her sister lived in the Ladies' Dormitory with 10 or 12 other women students.

In 1860 Clara Waever opened a tiny shop in Copenhagen, stocked it with a few simple embroidery fabrics and her own designs, and eventually found other artists to design for her. It was the beginning of one of the best-known needlework shops in the world. Now merged with the Eva Rosenstand Corporation, the Clara Waever firm has kept its own designs, as has Rosenstand. A museum holding all the designs of the two firms will be opened shortly in Copenhagen, and a book covering this is also being published.

"In the evenings the girls did all kinds of handwork, and they were taught hardanger by the college president, J. N. Kildahl, and his wife, both of whom did hardanger. It was from that sister that Marie learned some of the stitches."

But it was to be years later, on a trip to Norway with the Concordia College Choir and visiting relatives in the Hardanger fjord area, that Marie Hanson found beautiful pieces of hardanger embroidery. There were piano scarves, bed sheets, pillow "shams," even decorative towels hung on a washstand to hide the soiled towels — all with the elegant open-work embroidery. Marie continued to work on it and in 1964 began to teach it to groups. Many of her students have gone on to teach the art to others. Susan reports that Marie Hanson, 85, is still busy with her needle.

"In fact, she just completed a three-yard altar cloth for her church!"

Completely different but also done with pulled threads and cut-out work was the Hedebo embroidery which originated around 1700 in the area just west of Copenhagen. This started as a fairly simple sewing called "window pane sewing" because of the open work, but in time became very difficult — and very beautiful.

There were many other "white seam" stitches. Holbein work had black double running stitches. *Naversøm* used drawn threads with a darning pattern; this was originally drawn over birch bark. *Svartstick* (black stitch) used lines of cross stitches, running stitches, satin stitches and double running stitches.

The one that is probably enjoying the greatest revival today is cross stitch. Not only the traditional sampler, but designs of all kinds are being produced, some of the best by the Danish Handcraft Guild. Sara Lawergren, a lovely woman who lives in Gotland, has created many charm-

In the Lofoten Islands off Norway, the saying is that fishing is best when the birch leaves are the size of a mouse's ear.

ing, easily adapted patterns for the DMC Company.

But my favorites of the revived embroideries are still the wool yarn works — bell pulls, wall hangings, table runners and pillows in rich "Scandinavian" colors with adaptations of old designs and symbols. These are worked on a mesh needlepoint canvas in one of several different stitches. The entire surface is usually covered.

In a small yarn shop in southern Sweden one day I asked, "Do you have any kits to be done in *klostersøm?*"

"Oh, no," replied the salesperson primly, "that is the Norwegian stitch."

Whether she meant, "We Swedes are not interested in THAT," or whether she meant, "We wouldn't presume to take their stitch away from them," I don't know. But it reminded me that the Swedes like to do the *tvistsöm* or long-legged cross stitch. This is a counted cross stitch in which the last stitch makes a long jump across two spaces; the finished piece has a textured look, like coarse weaving. Swedes like bright, cheerful colors and use many figures in their designs.

Norwegian Klostersøm

61

The "Norwegian stitch" — *klostersom* — is like the gobelin stitch in needlepoint: vertical stitches side by side create a square and the pattern is made up of these squares. Subtle shadings and unexpected jewel-like accent colors distinguish many of these. Although it is possible to build remarkable scenes with this stitch, it is at its best in intricate variations of the old geometric patterns and the rich old colors.

Another popular stitch for geometric designs is the double cross stitch done in heavy yarn on coarse mesh. This is also known as star stitch, diamond stitch, Smyrna stitch and leviathan stitch.

Knitting

But for all the lovely handcrafts, if you had a Scandinavian grandmother it's probably her knitting you remember best.

They knit, often from the age of five or six. Little girls in pigtails and wooden shoes knit as they anxiously watched the family's cows at pasture. They knit while they walked. They knit while they waited for the kettle to boil. They counted out intricate designs on mittens and socks and never seemed to lose their place.

The Vikings knit — yes, the men themselves. They brought back patterns from their travels and when they settled on a far-off coast their knitting started traditions there. Norwegians who settled on the Faroe and Shetland Islands brought knitting crafts with them. Today Shetland patterns are definitely Nordic in origin. No dyes are used; the yarn is the same color as it came off the sheep.

Fair Isle knitting is believed to be Spanish in origin. The Vikings may have brought it from their forays in the south. Some think the patterns were taken from the clothing of the corpses that washed ashore from the Spanish Armada.

Trees, reindeer, the eight-pointed star, ropes and anchors (in the form of cables) all find their way into Norwegian knitting patterns. The white of the snow is important as background, with designs worked in dark shades of red, green, brown and blue.

Norwegian knitting was likely passed on to Sweden, where the designs became more sophisticated. In Denmark, knitting was unknown until the 15th century, when a.group of stocking knitters was imported from Holland to knit stockings for Danish royalty. Even today there is a strong Dutch influence in Danish knitting.

Straw Weaving

"Wheat straw is the fiber of life. Creating traditional ornaments of straw, a creation of life from the soil, using one's hands, is truly an exciting and worthwhile craft.... "

Oliver E. Strand
Extension Agronomist
University of Minnesota

Working with grain to create ornaments began centuries ago. In Europe all grain was called "corn" and straw ornament weavings in pagan times had a religious significance, and so evolved the name, "corn dollies."

In pre-Viking Scandinavia it was believed that a spirit lived in the grain. To insure a good crop the next year, a few stalks of grain were saved from the last sheaf, giving the spirit a home until the following spring. This was the origin of the sheaf of grain put out for the winter birds, though now this is a Christmas custom. These held-over grain stalks may also have been woven into ornamental shapes and forms.

Jeannette Nelson Starr of Minneapolis, a teacher of wheat-weaving and author of "Fun With Straw" and "More Fun With Straw," says the "corn dollies" were also thank offerings. Now they have become a symbol of good luck and prosperity.

One of the favorite Scandinavian straw figures is the rooster. That bird, according to Scandinavian folklore, had magic powers that would even keep lightning from striking the home. Scandinavian homes often have rooster weathervanes and even some very old churches have a rooster atop their steeples, signifying watchfulness. And the figure of a rooster in the kitchen is almost certain to improve the cooking!

Grain stalks to be used in weaving must be cut in the field before it is combined. Later the grain becomes too ripe and is difficult to weave. The portion above the first joint is used for plaiting and weaving. The covering sheath must be removed; the grain stalk is soaked in cool water for at least 30 minutes and then kept moist. Stalks that are too dry make weaving difficult.

For more information on the wheat-weaving books, write Starrco, 5843 Portland Avenue South, Minneapolis, Minnesota 55417.

From "More Fun With Straw" by Jeannette Nelson Starr, used by permission.

5.

Folk Costumes

Scandinavian folk costumes puzzle Americans. Some even ask, "Do they dress like this in the Scandinavian countries?" Visitors return with pictures of large family gatherings — say, a wedding or festival — where many are wearing colorful folk costumes. Some are similar to others, others are completely different. Here, too, more and more men and women are saying, "I'd like to have a Norwegian (or Swedish, or Danish) folk costume."

It's not as simple as going to a store and buying one.

Traditionally speaking, this colorful attire should be called "folk clothing" rather than "costume." For this is what they are, the clothing worn by common folk of years past when they went to church or dressed for other festive affairs.

Norwegians call it a *bunad,* Swedes *folkdräkt,* Danes *klaededrägt.* Today the *bunad* or *dräkt,* either handed down in a family or constructed in traditions centuries old, are worn on festive occasions in the community they represent. Or they may be worn on a festive occasion in other parts of the country or other parts of the world. It is a way of saying, "By my dress you can see that I am from this particular district; I'm proud of my home area and this is my way of establishing contact with others who may have come from there."

Two things are important: that the dress conform in the greatest degree possible to the style historically and traditionally worn in the particular district it represents; and that it be reserved for festive occasions. Using the folk dress in any other way breaks with the original purpose of the clothing in old times.

In a sense the folk costume is a holdover from the days of class distinction.

For centuries, all but a small percentage of Scandinavians were country dwellers. They made their living as landowners, farmers, tenant farmers, hired hands or *torpare,* hired hands who received a small plot of land as part of their pay. Unwritten laws, as well as many government directives, decreed their rights and their limitations, their "place in life," if you will. These extended even to the type of clothing they wore, the material, style and color. So proscribed was the dress for each social class that one could tell at a glance whether a man was a farm laborer, *bonde,* (small farmer), merchant, pastor, military man, member of the landed gentry or noble. Thus in Selma Lagerlof's "Lilliecrona's Home," Sven Lilliecrona, the smith, had come from a long line of pastors and so his dress was decreed to be that of a gentleman. But when he came riding to Svenskog he dressed as a peasant, right to the close-fitting, stiff coat of fur. So effective was his disguise that no one recognized him and Maia Lisa alone guessed that it might be he.

The nobility and the gentry could dress in the latest styles from the continent. Another Lagerlof book includes a description of a funeral in Varmland that might have taken place in the early 1800s. In "Gösta Berling's Saga," Ferdinand Uggla's widow wanted his funeral to be as joyful an occasion as a wedding. So the author describes all the buckles and brooches and pearls and golden bracelets that adorned all the women. They wore ostritch feathers in their bonnets and their gowns were of satin, their shawls of thin silk. Nor were the men any less splendid. They came in coats with gilded buttons, shirts with swelling ruffles and vests of brocade and embroidered velvet. There was no homespun here. These were not peasants.

But for the poor *bonde* family, holding to the same traditional dress year after year meant that it was necessary to spin, weave and sew new clothing only when the old wore out. And since the attire dictated by tradition was that worn only to church on Sundays (everyday working clothes were similar mostly out of necessity), the men's coats and women's dresses lasted for years and were often passed on to sons and daughters.

Outside of seafaring men and soldiers, few country dwellers ever left their immediate area, their home valley. Men and women were born, wed, raised families and died without ever leaving the confines of their own *dal* or *socken*. So the clothing of the immediate area became more and more alike. Small variations, like a type of button or a certain style of cuff, became indigenous to the area where they evolved. Tradition grew strong. Change was frowned upon.

~~~~~~

"Shortly after her marriage Catherine adopted the antique costume of the country, which the nobility had discarded in favor of more modern fashions, and no mockery, such as that in which her brother Charles indulged, could make her change. Many other ladies, friends of Catherine's, followed her example and also left off wearing superfluous ornaments."

- From an account of St. Catherine of Sweden, who died in 1381.

~~~~~~

Periodically, the government would take action against excessive spending on lavish clothing and other luxuries. In Sweden in the early 1700s, for instance, laws were passed against superfluity in dress among all classes. Parish pastors, who represented the authority of the state, often railed against new ideas, like the use of "bought" fabrics. In 1728 some young girls in one Swedish parish were given eight days in jail on bread and water for wearing too elaborate caps. And later, in Västergotland, it was decreed that the woolen cloth in men's jackets should be "of the same color as that which the sheep wore."

For the poor, humility was deemed the virtue next to godliness, and homespun was humble.

The influence of the Church certainly helped influence the traditional dress. For in order not to be shamed as a non-believer, every adult had to attend communion at least once a year. Since "church clothes" were obligatory, every man and woman must have the attire that had become traditional in that parish.

In some parts of Sweden the style of dress was so tied to the church year that it changed for different Sundays. The very fanciest outfit was worn on high church holidays, plainer ones for lesser holidays. For *domsöndagen* they wore somber clothes and on Good Friday mourning clothes. All of these were of a particular pattern, which might vary from parish to parish. It was said that in Dalarna there were such strict traditions for church wear on certain Sundays that one almost needed a special almanac to keep track!

Not everyone had all the outfits, of course. But it must be remembered that not everyone was poor, even of the common rural folk. There were rich farmers and others fairly well-to-do. They might wear homespun skirts and aprons made from the linen of flax they had themselves grown, but many also had fine silver and metal jewelry. In the prosperous Hardanger area of Norway, for example, there was the large spangled *solje* brooch. On the day she was married, a young woman was permitted to wear this among her smaller brooches, for it was the symbol of matrons. For all their somber colors, older women wore an abundance of chains, brooches and disks (as in the *solje*).

A Sunday in a remote Norwegian valley was a medley of homespun wool skirts and trousers, embroidered vests both bright and dark, coats of a particular cut, skirts and blouses with elaborate stitchery, possibly red knitted stockings and boots or shoes with shining buckles.

The amazing thing is that today, three or four centuries later, you may go to the same valley and see precisely the same outfit, right down to the tiniest tucks on the bodice and the minute embroidery on the braid trim.

How is this possible?

As early as 1700, people of other classes began showing an interest in the dress of the common man, finding it unusual and "picturesque." It became fashionable for nobles and their ladies to have a "country costume" which they wore to balls much as we would wear a costume to a costume party. When the 1800s brought a resurgence of pride in things Scandinavian, the folk costume, which was associated with old-time culture and tradition, began to gain real respectability.

But the 1800s brought other changes. Sparked by the American and French Revolutions, changes were brought about that included land reform. Ownerships were rearranged to put lands together and owners were encouraged to live on their land. This meant that sometimes long-standing settled areas were severed. On top of this, industrialization brought new goods and it was no longer necessary to produce everything at home. Cotton materials and ready-made goods became available. By the mid-1800s, especially in Sweden and Denmark, little was left of the colorful country folk wear.

But at the same time that it was being discarded or packed away, artists and historians were showing interest in it. Artists traveled through the countrysides painting local people in their old costumes. Others began collecting as much of the old home-made garb and household articles as they could find, that they might not be lost to future generations. Notable among these was Artur Hazelius of Sweden, whose collection formed the nucleus of the *Nordiska museet* or Nordic Museum in Stockholm.

In Sweden by 1900 there was a strong romantic interest in the *bondedräkt* and people began creating their own costumes along that style, putting modern blouses with old skirts and maybe adding a striped apron. But more and more it was felt that if these expressions of a past culture were to be preserved, they should be authentic. The folk dress, said those who were truly interested, should be worn exactly as it had been worn at one time in a precise community. It should be "apparel with a local individuality and distinction." There sprang up organizations like *Ungdomsringen för*

From the dolls of Røhnaug Petterssen
Norsk Folkemuseum

bygdekultur ("Young People's Circle for Home Area Culture"). Between the two World Wars, no less than 700 *hembygdsföreningar* (home area societies) were organized. All of these have contributed to researching folk costumes of their areas and preserving authenticity both of design and use.

Similar steps were taken in Norway, where the isolation of many of the mountain areas kept the *bunad* in use to a much later date. In Finland peasant dress was greatly simplified, probably during its long rule by Russia, when every effort was made to stamp out Finnish nationalism. Green was a popular color for aprons and also stockings. Aprons, however, eventually lost their individuality and were even missing from the costume. Silver jewelry, buckles and buttons were plentiful.

Some old Danish homes had a special garden called a "bleach green" where new linen was laid out on the grass to be bleached by the sun and weather.

Because of its proximity to the continent, Denmark adopted continental styles earlier. A flat, level land without geographically isolated areas, it never had the wealth of indigenous costumes that Norway and Sweden had. Nor did it have an uninterrupted tradition of folk wear; its use died out at one time. But in Denmark, too, it is being revived. There are still many styles, especially in the islands, and they are charming and original. For example, why did a bride in the Fano Islands wear a little mirror in the back of her flowered cap? They called it the "all-seeing eye," whatever that may have meant. Also, on the day she was married she had the right to leave the third button of her blouse unbuttoned.

Danes often used "cooked pleats" in their garments. The wool material was gathered in back and on the sides, leaving the front plain where the skirt fastener would be covered by an apron. The pleating was tacked at regular intervals. The garment was then sprinkled with water, wrapped in muslin and put in the oven after the bread baking was finished and the heat diminishing. The skirt was literally cooked, and the results resembled accordion pleating.

Simple white bonnets which could be washed easily were worn under the outer bonnet. For the same reason a white scarf was knotted around the neck. Aprons for Sunday were often of checked silk. Hedebo had a lovely cap with "Hedebo embroidery"; for a time that lovely embroidery almost died out but now it is often used on dresses and household linens as well as caps for folk wear.

For both men and women, caps and headscarves were not only proper but very practical for the houses of that time were drafty and cold. Danish men wore knitted caps resembling the traditional nightcap — a double cap in which the outer one was long, ending in a tassel. The inner one fit the head closely, with patterned knitting aimed at warming the head. On occasion a man might even wear a silk top hat over his traditional cap. The caps and scarves were the last of the folkwear to be abandoned when country folk stopped wearing their traditional garb.

Iceland has never had strong local districts marked by isolation from the rest of the country. Consequently it has one traditional folk costume for the entire country, the only Nordic country to have a true "national costume," although others are attempting to establish one.

Partly responsible for the revival of the old attire was a new interest in the old time music and folk dances which had begun to die out in the 19th century. With the turn of the century and growing emphasis on old Nordic culture, dancers again jigged and swayed to the old country music. This in turn led to interest in the old folk dress, exactly as it had been.

And today, grandchildren of those who emigrated here tap their feet in silver-buckled shoes, red or white or black stockings, aprons and bobbing white caps.

To Acquire Your Own Costume

"Yes, you could put any black skirt, white blouse, white apron and red vest together and call it a Norwegian costume," agreed Gloria Pederson.

"But," she added emphatically, "then call it a *costume,* not a *bunad!*"

Pederson and Pat Kelly, both of Tacoma, Washington, are two of a growing number of people in this country who are encouraging the emphasis on keeping folk dress for both men and women authentic.

The Norwegian word *bunad,* Pederson explained, refers to one native garb that represents one specific valley, hamlet or area in Norway. It has been researched through old paintings, museum acquisitions and musty depths of old trunks. It has been given official sanction by cultural groups like *Husfliden* to represent that area as THE native folk habit.

The same concepts and restrictions are generally true in Sweden and Denmark, too. But lets use the well-known Hardanger dress for women as an example of what goes into a *bunad.*

In the Hardanger area of Norway, the beautiful festival dress never did go out of use. Today it is worn to confirmations, weddings and, of course, on the 17th of May. (Norwegians tell of the World War II years when their land was occupied by Nazi troops. Because it was impossible to buy new clothing, the old folk wear was brought out of trunks; it was warm and long-wearing. The Nazis, seeing the folk outfits as an expression of Norwegian resistance, fumed at the sight. The angrier they grew, the more the Norwegians wore the garb.)

71

The Hardanger *bunad,* as described by Pat Kelly, has a bright red vest of wool with rose trim. The skirt is of black wool with three bands of black velvet around the bottom. The *ekte Norsk* vest trim has in it gold, representing Christ's crown of thorns; red roses, representing blood dripping on the flower, and green, representing life. No other braid should be substituted. (If one is unable to get this, small black velvet ribbon should be used.) Shirts (blouses) of all Norwegian *bunader* (plural form) are cut from the same pattern; variations come in the collars and cuffs and their trim. Hardanger embroidery, a form of open work on even-weave material, distinguishes this blouse as well as the apron. It may be of cotton or linen. The belt is of red wool with certain added sashes, embroidered and trimmed with braid and silver. There is a breastplate, and while the rest of the dress may be identical to others, embroidery of the beaded breastplate should always be in one's own design.

The folk dress for men is just as carefully detailed. To put together such an outfit is no small undertaking. And with hundreds of separate areas with their own folk dress, there is no way a shop in this country could stock them all.

There are three ways in which you may obtain such an outfit or one representing another area.

First, you may order a completed one from Norway. (Addresses for ordering from the Scandinavian countries are given at the end of this chapter.) It will take up to two years to get it and at this writing will cost anywhere from $1200 to $2000, depending on the amount of work in it. When considering the cost, remember that these outfits are made of lasting materials and are meant to be passed on from one generation to the next. They are made with wide seams so they may be altered to fit changing figures.

Secondly, you may order the pieces, cut and embroidered, and sew the outfit together yourself.

Thirdly, you may order the pieces cut out, with directions for the embroidering and finishing. "Norwegians think we're crazy to attempt it all ourselves," smiled Gloria. "Over there, the person who does the embroidery usually doesn't do the cutting or tailoring." All the processes are done in the flourishing home industries there.

There is another option, one which many folk-dancing, rosemaling and other groups have chosen. That is to create a costume more like the everyday dress of the common Scandinavian folk of times past. This can be a happy, colorful statement of ethnic fellowship. But this would not be one of the *bunader* but rather, for example, a "dance costume."

Whatever your choice, remember that no folk dress is to be worn carelessly. Festive *bunader* or *folkdräkt* should be reserved for truly festive occasions. Purists insist that if they are to be true to tradition they should be worn only to church and at weddings.

And whether the dress has been passed down to you from a relative or constructed by ancient traditions, it's well to remember this advice from the

Skedevi costume
from
Östergötland

authors of a colorful Swedish book, *"Folkdräkter,"* Inga Arno Berg and Gunnel Hazelius Berg.

"All who wear the folk dress," write the Bergs, "should know something of its history and have some relationship with the area from which the costume comes. When you dress in folk wear, you become a representative of the region it represents and should show your respect by wearing it in a proper manner."

If you're not certain where your ancestors came from in Scandinavia, it might be good to spend some time on family research before you choose a costume. Of course, you can always choose one that just happens to appeal to you. But in that case, be sure to learn all you can about the area it represents so that you may be a good ambassador of the region.

Some feel a "national costume" should be adopted to simplify things. Others say that the official committees who set standards for the costumes are more hard-lined about detail than the communities where the costumes originated ever were.

One Norwegian writer, for instance, uses the example of a woman from a certain region wearing a green blouse with her *bunad.* It would be said that she is not wearing the correct *bunad* because the blouse should be white.

This, he comments, is unfortunate because "there was a much wider variation in costumes of the past.

"In many ways the officially correct bunad is an attempt to stagnate tradition which is always changing. Often the country women would buy fine ribbons and material when on a trip to town and these would be sewn onto their costumes. There are some lovely examples of waistcoats with colored velvet edges in various museum collections, but these would never be accepted as the correct *bunad* from the district."

Still, the supervision has corrected a condition existing earlier in this century. When tourism in Scandinavia became popular, all kinds of postcards were issued showing young women in colorful "native" costume. There was more fantasy than fact in them — the model might be wearing parts of four or five different costumes!

For information on how to order a Norwegian *bunad,* contact any *Husfliden* (Home Industries) shop in Norway. The address for the Bergen shop is Husfliden i Bergen, Post Box 416, 5001 Bergen, Norway.

For information about Swedish provincial wear, write Hemslöjdsforbundet, Storagaten 29, Stockholm 114 S36.

In Denmark, write the Danish Handcraft Guild, Vimmelskafget No. 38, DK-1161, Copenhagen K; or Danske Folkedanseres Draktudvalg, care of Mrs. Agnes Jørgensen, Smedefort 9, DK-6340, Krusa, Denmark. Enclosing a dollar for postage is appreciated.

Isolation and Early Travel

In our mobile society, it's difficult to understand the isolation that existed in Scandinavian communities of the past.

Norway's, of course, is easier to see. The impenetrable mountains and rock-walled fjords still isolate many. Denmark's level land and relatively small area never presented quite the same problems that the other two lands experienced.

But even in Sweden it was not until the 19th century that "ordinary people" were able to travel at all.

The Nordic Museum in Stockholm points out that in medieval times travelers all rode horses or went by foot. For the most part they were royal messengers or pilgrims bound for a holy place and living off any generosity they could find. There were no roads that would have accommodated a coach, and such vehicles as did exist were primitive and uncomfortable.

Any nobleman's party or any of the king's men could pound on any peasant's door and demand lodging for the night; it was the law. By the end of the 16th century the peasants were growing bitter about this compulsory quartering. Attempts to abolish it and instead establish inns had proven unsuccessful.

But the 17th century brought changes. A central state had been formed and it demanded networks of communication to hold it together. Roads were gradually improved.

And Queen Christina's Travelers' Ordinance of 1649 finally led to a workable system of conveyance. Inns were to be set up along the routes. It still fell on the peasant as an obligation to convey travelers to the next stop. But now travelers were to pay for their transport at a fixed rate, and so the peasants were paid for their services. Foreigners at the time were surprised at how easily they traveled in Sweden, even though it could take a great deal of time.

Roads continued to be improved during the 17th and 18th centuries. An ordinance in 1649 prescribed that the roads should be measured with cords so that "all miles should be of equal length" and that "certain stones and indications should be set up at the end of every mile." Now it was possible to know how far one had traveled and how much one should pay. The inns were not far apart, sometimes as close as one to one and a half Swedish miles along the road. (The Swedish mile is roughly equal to six English miles or 10 kilometers.)

And though the conveyance system lasted for almost 300 years, traveling this way was still expensive for the ordinary Swede. One Swedish mile cost about a day's wages. So, almost as it was in the Middle Ages, most travelers at the beginning of the 1800s were officials on government service or wealthy members of the nobility or upper middle class.

The 19th century brought a revolution in traveling. It began with the Göta Canal and other canals on which steamers, fast and affordable, began to travel. In 1862 the main railroad line to the west was completed. The railway network was constantly expanded. The State assumed responsibility for the main lines; private railway associations developed local service to link up small centers of population outside the area served by the main line. These local lines were often narrow gauge. Soon it was possible to travel from Stockholm to Malmo in one day instead of the ten days required by coach.

But the most important aspect was, perhaps, the fact that the comparatively cheap class fare at last allowed the general public a chance to travel.

Still, traveling for pleasure took time and money. With the advent of the bicycle, the working class and young people had a handy way of getting around. In 1938, when a bill was passed granting two week vacations for all, cycling was greatly encouraged. Bicycling holidays with tents became popular and the number of camping sites and youth hostels have continued to increase.

Since the end of World War II cars have increasingly taken over the role of the cycle as the individual's means of getting around.

"But we are aware," said the representative who had arranged a travel exhibit for the Museum, "that there is a price to be paid for the personal freedom associated with the possession of a car. The atmosphere is polluted, the countryside scarred by motorways. Collective tranpsort cannot compete. To travel by rail is expensive and only really possible for those who live in the right places — where the trains stop. We can afford to take charter flights to destinations outside Sweden, but to travel by air in Sweden is still too expensive for most of us. Choice of means of travel is still a matter of money."

6.

Music and Dance

When we think of ethnic Scandinavian music, it's probably the *spelman*, the fiddler, who comes to mind. He's the one who provided the music at social gatherings and, with his fiddle tucked securely under his chin, led the wedding procession to and from the church.

But ballad singing and folk dancing were very much the entertainment of the people in years past. The reason most of us know so little about it is that much of the Scandinavian immigrant population sprang from the pietistic movement that looked on the fiddle and the dance as the straight road to hell. The same mores were part of strict, church-centered Scandinavian communities in this country. Consequently, much of the color and flavor of the North's country music was lost for a time and is not as familiar as, say, the Slavic music and dance.

Actually, music has existed for thousands of years in the North countries. Archaeological finds include bronze horns estimated to be 3000 years old and 2000-year old bone flutes very much like the flutes in use today. From the Viking age have come cow and ram horns, and we can only guess at how they were used.

One of the finest summaries of Nordic folk music and dance is one published recently by the Nordic Heritage Museum in Seattle and its director, Marianne Forssblad. They have kindly agreed to share it with us, and this entire section is taken from the Museum's publication. (Here the term "Nordic" is used, rather than "Scandinavian," referring to the five Nordic countries with which this museum deals.)

Until a few generations ago the Nordic countries **were** primarily agrarian societies, and folk music is deeply rooted in this rural life style. The wooden flute and the horn were typical of the musical instruments of the summer mountain farms *(fäbod* or *seter* of Sweden and Norway). In order to free the land closest to the village for growing crops, young girls and older women brought the cattle up into the mountains where they stayed over the summer producing cheese and butter. Long birch-bark horns were used to play a variety of tunes, each of which had a special function in the daily routine of the farm, such as calling the animals.

Vocal music was also an integral part of Nordic culture. People sang at work and at play, normally without instrumental accompaniment. Ballad texts have been known since the Middle Ages, but there are very few singers today who can render such ballads in the traditional manner.

Rural Nordic society had many musicians with a variety of instruments, by far the most common being the fiddle (Swedish *fiol*). Before the introduction of the violin, other bowed stringed instruments existed, and Nordic folk music is definitely shaped by its intimate relationship to the bowing of strings. In Upland, Sweden, a keyed fiddle *(nyckelharpa)* which dates back to the Middle Ages became the popular instrument. Rather than being fingered as a violin, the strings are stopped by wooden pegs. In recent years the key-fiddle has regained its popularity, and courses in instrument-building are offered. Norway's national instrument is the Hardanger fiddle *(hardingfele)* which, like the key-fiddle, employs a set of unbowed under-strings which vibrate in resonance with the bowed strings. Highly ornamented, this remarkable instrument is common to western and southern Norway, whereas in eastern Norway the regular fiddle *(flatfele)* prevails. The national instrument of Finland is a form of psaltery called *kantele.* It originally had five strings, but during the 19th century its size and number of strings increased. Unlike the fiddle, the *kantele* was not used for dance music.

The principal function of the fiddler in rural Scandinavia was to provide music for dancing at social gatherings and weddings, and even to play at funerals and other ceremonies. Some fiddlers were full-time musicians, but the majority were crofters, farm hands, craftsmen or soldiers. Many built their own instruments so form and construction often varied. An unusual example is the wooden-shoe fiddle *(träskofiol)* of Scania, southern Sweden.

Most country fiddlers did not read music, but played by ear, learning their repertoire from older musicians, for true folk music cannot be transmitted by written note; to capture the indigenous spirit and folk character it must be passed on by ear from human to human.

In the second half of the 19th century a stern pietistic movement made serious inroads in many parts of Scandinavia. Preachers condemned dancing and the fiddle as the work of the Devil, so that in many areas instrumental folk music was totally extinguished. The transformation from an agrarian to an industrial society with the resultant migration from rural to urban centers also had a devastating effect on the old folk culture.

As traditional musical and dance forms were replaced by modern popular idioms at the turn of the century, it was feared that the older indigenous music would disappear altogether. To counteract these developments fiddlers' competitions were organized. In Sweden these were soon replaced by non-competitive gatherings of folk musicians called *spelmansstämmor.* Fiddlers' ensembles *(spelmanslag)* are also a typical Swedish phenomenon. During the past quarter of a century many such groups have toured Europe and the United States.

Many young people in the Nordic countries today are actively engaged in perpetuating traditional music and dance. It must be remembered that it is thanks to a few staunch tradition-bearers in "folklore pockets" such as Dalarna in Sweden and Telemark in Norway, who have kept their unbroken heritage of folk fiddling alive, that the legacy of authentic ethnic instrumental music has been passed on to the present generation.

Nordic dance in its oldest form dates back to the Middle Ages. Line and circle dancing spread northward from Provence, France, through the chivalrous culture. From the courts of Scandinavia these dances found their way to the rural population, where they became colored by local tradition so that distinct regional variables developed.

An unbroken living tradition in Medieval dance, unique in western Europe, exists today on the Faroe Islands. Musical instruments are not used; the dancers sing ancient ballads as they move about in a ring with a repetitive step. In the church of Orslev, Denmark, such a line dance is depicted on a fresco painting dating back to the early 15th century.

Traditional dancing in the Nordic countries today is basically socio-recreational in nature. In contrast to folk dances in many other parts pf the world, Nordic dances require partners of the opposite sex. Furthermore, they involve couples in fast rotation. *(Example: old time waltz.)*

The folk dances also tend to express local or national characteristics. Danish folk dance reflects to a great degree the country's proximity to the Continent and the British Isles. More than 400 contras, squares and other dances have been collected and recorded. The oldest dances of Norway include the *gangar, springar, halling* and *pols,* which originated in the 1500s and 1600s. More recent figure dances *(turdansar)* are primarily of 19th century origin. Song-dances *(songdansar),* popular with all Norwegian folk dance clubs *(leikarringar)* are derived from the Faroese dance form.

The folk dances of Finland reflect the bi-cultural history of that country, with pure Finnish as well as Finland-Swedish forms. Many formal Finnish folk dances are in the polka rhythm which is a fairly recent development. Most of the folk dances of Sweden, however, are of a much greater age, with a predominance of the triple-meter *polska* dating from the 16th century and found in countless variations throughout the land. With the introduction of the accordion in the 19th century, the *polska* was supplanted by newer dances such as the *waltz, schottis* and *polka.* The *polska* did survive in the form of the *hambo,* which is still popular today. These later dance forms are generally referred to as old-time dance *(gammaldans)* and are often associated with accordion music. Dances originating in the pre-industrial era (before 1850) are associated with fiddle music and are generally classified as *bygdedans,* best rendered as regional ethnic dance. Their current popularity in Sweden can be attributed to the revival of fiddle music around 1970.

Many regional festivals throughout this country include Scandinavian singing and dancing. If you would like to know more about groups fostering this culture, contact Scandinavian organizations in your area (Vasa, Sons of Norway, etc.) or write the American-Scandinavian museum nearest you (addresses for four of these are in the section on "Exploring Further.")

7.

Holidays

In pagan times people of the North kept track of time by means of calendar sticks. Notches marked off the days between the longest and shortest days of the year. In between lay symbols of all the crop and farming lore that had evolved in that *bygd* or area for generations.

With the coming of the first priest-missionaries and the establishment of far-flung parishes, the Church needed a way to remind illiterate farmers and peasants of the holy days; on some they were to abstain from work, on others fasting was in order. So the stick became the "mass staff," with carved symbols signifying the days that honored saints or sacred events.

Now, centuries later, with all the upheavals of religious turn-arounds and political wars, those holy days are still the basis of Scandinavian holidays. The observance may have grown more worldly and superficial, the traditions may overshadow the origins, but in Scandinavia "holiday" translates very literally into "holy day."

Your grandparents brought some of those traditions with them, though for Norwegians the most festive day outside of Christmas has likely been a secular holiday, May 17. The day marks not the relatively recent separation from Sweden, but the 1814 constitution drawn up at Eidsvold. And though Sweden ruled Norway until 1905, it recognized that constitution, which gave Norway a limited independence after centuries of Danish rule.

Christmas, of course, was the crowning celebration in the "old country" and among immigrant Scandinavians as well. One Swedish writer, commenting that children of long ago had no Advent calendars with "little doors" to open, went on to say, "Instead, the whole stretch of time before Christmas was one long, living calendar. Each day one carried out one or more of the pre-Christmas preparations. So the days themselves, one might say, were like the little doors of today's Advent calendars."

But there were others.

On one of the calendar sticks in the Norwegian Folk Museum in Oslo is a symbol resembling a candlestick, marking Candlemas Day, February 2. Back in Catholic times it was a day when the priest distributed candles to his parishioners as a symbolic gesture to guard them against the power of the devil. The day also commemorated the purification of Mary, mother of Jesus, after his birth.

Although no longer practiced by the Church, there was a time even in Protestant tradition when a woman who had given birth had to go through a small ceremony to be received back into the active life of the parish. The history of Ljungby parish in Sweden recalls it:

" 'Church-taking-in' was a ceremony in which a woman, after childbirth, was taken back into the life of the congregation. She would go to the front of the church and the pastor would read specially appointed prayers. After this there would be a feast in the home. The mother would show that she had regained her strength by preparing and serving lots of food, or by taking part in the dancing that followed." Just what a new mother needed, especially if she already had a large brood of children!

Some holiday traditions came about through some convoluted logic. The Feast of the Annunciation, March 25, was called *"Varfrudagen"* in Sweden, literally "Our Lady's Day." The common pronunciation became *"vafferdagen."* Along the way it turned into *"vaffeldagen"* ("waffle day") and it became customary to eat waffles on that day! This explains the origin of the heart-shaped waffle irons you see in Scandinavian gift stores; the waffles were to commemorate the heart of the Virgin Mary.

Scandinavians might be said to have their own Mardi Gras. There were many customs associated with the period immediately before Lent. Feasting and gaiety were the order, since the next 40 days (in the centuries of Catholic rule) would be somber and meatless.

Their Fat Tuesday originated in the times of the early Church when the people grumbled at having to go without meat all 40 days of Lent (the 40 days representing Christ's fast in the wilderness). Finally the authorities permitted a piece or two of fat pork each Tuesday. The Tuesday before

Santa Maria Church,
Visby, Gotland

While the cross is the most common symbol on the old church spires of Scandinavia, it comes as a surprise to see a rooster crowning some of them, like this one on Santa Maria Church in Visby on Gotland. Unlike the rooster weathervane on homes, a good luck symbol, the rooster on a church symbolizes eternal vigilance. It was a rooster that reminded the disciple Peter of the words of Jesus, "Before the cock crows twice, you will have denied me three times."

Lent was *fettisdag,* with some special sweet buns called *fettisdagbullar,* still eaten today but called *semlor.*

On the night before Good Friday (Maundy Thursday) and the night before All Saints Day (Hallowe'en), the people's fear of witches sent icy chills through any hapless traveler who had to be out after dark. In Norway witches would certainly be seen soaring off to the snowy mountains of Dovre, while in Sweden they mounted their brooms and headed for Blåkulla, always to rendezvous with the devil. As the superstitions have faded, tradition has preserved gentler versions. Children dress up as *påsk-kärringer* (Easter Witches) and go from house to house wishing everyone a happy Easter and stopping long enough to collect treats. Danish children used to wake their parents with birch sticks decorated with colored feathers. The sticks may be a reminder of the "Easter switch," a long-ago Good Friday rite in which the lord of the manor gave each of the family and the servants a few lashes with a birch branch to remind them of the sufferings of Christ.

In some areas great bonfires were burned on Easter Eve to frighten away the witches. But this was not common all over, for in some areas there was not enough burnable wood anyway, let alone enough to waste in this manner. Too, pastors were having a hard enough time weaning their flock away from belief in witchcraft and other superstitions, and they preached strongly against the bonfires.

Easter itself was more of a church celebration than a home celebration, but there were always the traditional foods — as many eggs as one could possibly eat for breakfast, and the smoked pork leg that had been saved from the Christmas butchering.

Pagan practices were at the heart of the Cuckoo Mass May 1, marked on the Norwegian calendar stick with a bird perched in a tree. In pre-Christian times it was believed that if the cuckoo's call was heard for the first time that spring from the north, one would become ill or die that year. (Note the resemblance to the belief of the Indians of Canada's west coast as in Margaret Craven's "I Heard the Owl Call My Name.") If the call was first heard from the south, the year would be favorable; if from the west, one would succeed, and if from the east, one would be lucky in love. Actually, the day — dedicated to a German saint named Valbor — is best known by the eve that precedes it. On Walpurgis Night, the last night of April, students officially welcome Spring, first with organized activities and later with eating and dancing that reach to the dawn. It's not one of the holidays that has survived with Scandinavians in this country.

Pentecost, a lesser holiday after Easter, commemorates the outpouring of the Holy Spirit on the followers of Christ. One of my treasured memories of Oslo is a cab ride in which the driver talked to me in slow Norwegian, I talked to him in fractured Swedish and we understood each other quite well. He and his family, he told me, were going to his wife's parents in Sweden "på Pingst" (on Pentecost). The word brought back a rush of memories; in my childhood, "Pingst" was a special time in spring crop lore. Am I right in remembering that the potatoes had to be planted by

"Pingst?"

One of the non-church holidays Scandinavian enjoy is the same as one of ours — April Fools Day. There's a little verse:

"April, April, din dumma sil,
Jag kan lura dig vart jag vill."

Or,

"April, April, you silly fish,
I can trick you however I wish."

If you grew up in a northern climate, locked for almost half the year in deep snow, biting winds and short, dark days, you should have no trouble understanding why spring and summer were— and are — almost worshipped by Scandinavians. In pagan times the beginning of the lengthening dark, bitter cold days was a sign that the spirits were again waking in the earth. There could have been no better time for the Christian religion to superimpose the festival of Christmas — unless it would have been at Midsummer, the day when everyone celebrated the long, glorious hours of warm daylight and burgeoning crops.

The immigrant Scandinavians brought their Misummer (always June 24) festivities along to the new land. The Swedes seem to celebrate it more than others, possibly because for the Norwegians it pales before the celebration a month earlier of their Constitution Day, May 17. (Danish Constitution Day is June 5, the day that King Frederick VII signed Denmark's first free constitution.)

Swedish communities here often erect a maypole on Midsummer Day and dancers in costume perform the old folk dances around it. Incidentally, the word *maj,* as in *majstäng* (maypole), has nothing to do with the month of May. *Maj* refers to greenery— leaves and branches and flowers that trim the pole. It is a joyous tribute to summer and the greening of the earth.

Denmark is one of the few countries that joins the United States in celebrating our Independence Day, and it has been doing so ever since 1904. For the most part, festivities are confined to Rebild Park in the north of Jutland. Here visiting Danish Americans and other Danes gather by the thousands to mark the good relations between the two countries.

If there are few memorable holidays between Midsummer and Christmas, it may be because the pressure of caring for the land, of planting and cultivating and harvesting in that short growing season, left little time for merrymaking. Haymaking and harvest went from dawn to dark in the days when both had to be done with a scythe and the women raked and tied the grain. In areas where wood was scarce, taking up peat for fuel was one of the summer chores. Peat, a dusty stuff in old moss bogs where the vegetable matter had partially carbonized, held a fire fairly well but smoked, smelled and left a great deal of ash.

Summer's long days also brought whole families out to the market days that were held in nearby towns, a time to sell grain and to buy and sell livestock

And when the harvest was at last finished, when the flax was in the drying shed, when the last threshing floor had been swept and the grain was ready for the mill, darkness and cold were already setting in. On St. Simon's Day, October 28, according to the calendar stick, the cattle were to be moved indoors for the winter. On St. Martin's Day, November 11, any farm animals that were not to be kept through the winter should be slaughtered — all, that is, except the Christmas pig. On St. Catherine's Day, November 25, women of the house should begin their spinning for the winter. On St. Thomas' Day, December 21, the Christmas ale should be brewed.

~~~~~~

In Sweden, and particularly in Skane, Nov. 11 is observed as St. Martin's Day. St. Martin, one of the earliest Christian prelates, died on that date. The legend goes that his diocese wanted to make him a bishop. But Martin, painfully shy and modest, wanted no part of it and hid in the goose pen when the Church fathers came to persuade him. But alas for Martin, the geese honked loudly and gave him away and a bishop he became. To this day the people of Skane eat goose on St. Martin's Day.

~~~~~~

But eight days before that, on December 13, came the day that marked the start of the Christmas preparations — St. Lucia's Day.

So familiar is the Lucia Day festivity in this country that we forget the festival as we know it is of fairly recent origin.

But like many other festivals its roots are in ancient times. Under the old calendar, the night of December 13 was considered the longest night of the year. Horrible beings from the bowels of the earth were believed to be afoot that night and the early Norsemen feasted and drank in their effort to call forth the sun god again. Soon they themselves began to dress in grotesque masks and strange clothes and went about frightening as many poor souls as they could. Their refreshments at the homes where they called were not coffee and Lucia buns, but *brannvin* (brandy) — *"lussesup"* (literally "cup of light"). Over the years it became the custom to serve this "cup of light" to the butcher, for this was the day on which he came to stick the Christmas pig.

How this old celebration of light merged with the legend of St. Lucia of Sicily is hard to say. Lucia, a beautiful young woman of Syracuse, was born in 283 and was converted to Christianity. When her mother fell ill, it is told, Lucia made a vow that if God would spare her mother's life she would forego marriage and remain a virgin. When her mother recovered, Lucia persuaded her to divide among the poor all the wealth and possessions that would have been Lucia's dowry.

Furious, the man to whom she was engaged reported her to the authorities. Since she was without dowry, they sought to force her into prostitution. Remarkably, she remained a virgin and even survived burning

Girl as Santa Lucia

at the stake. But in the year 303 she died by the executioner's sword.

Did the Vikings bring back tales of Lucia? Did the early missionaries tell her story? Was it the similarity between her name and the word for light (*ljus*) that drew the Scandinavians, especially the Swedes, so deeply to her legend? One of the tales most often told is that during a famine in Värmland a brightly lighted ship came sailing in on Lake Vänern. It was Lucia, bringing vast gifts of food. Was it the memory of the pagan goddess Freya, who was said to bring mead in a golden horn as harbinger of a good year to come?

Although there are records of earlier observances, the custom of the eldest daughter of the house serving coffee and saffron buns on the morning of December 13 seems to have started around 1700 among rich farmers and estate owners in west Sweden. At first Lucia was depicted as an angel with wings, but in time she was simply the eldest daughter in a white gown with a crown of blazing candles on her head. From there the custom spread. Today many churches and lodges in United States and Canada hold Lucia fests.

Whatever the origins, in its present form it is a charming family observance. It is a time to pause in what has become a hectic race before Christmas. It is a glance back at a simpler time, a sharing, an expression of love and a harbinger of the real Festival of Light.

By St. Lucia's Day, any farm work to be done before Christmas was to be completed. Now the preparations began inside the house.

Writing for a Stockholm newspaper, *Dagens Nyheter,* Lars-Ingmar Karlsson recently interviewed two elderly sisters who grew up many years ago on a large farm in Halland in southern Sweden. Their account of getting ready for Christmas is probably much like that your Grandmother would have told you.

Since they had help both in the house and with the cattle, Astrid and Nanny explained, the people of the household usually handled all the work alone. But early in December it was time to do one of the biggest clothes washings of the year, and so the "washer-women" came. Each of these two women lived alone in a small *stuga* in the neighborhood and made the rounds of the farms, "helping out."

The washing took two full days. On the first day they scrubbed the clothes, standing at a huge tub filled with steaming hot water. By evening they moved the clothes into a huge round tub, big as a dining table, and there they soaked overnight. In the morning the water was poured out and the tub loaded on a wagon and hauled to a nearby spring where the water ran even through the snow. Here the clothes were rinsed, then brought home to hang on lines and fences to freeze dry.

Next came the butchering. Always before Christmas a pig must be butchered and often a calf as well.

"Part of the meat went into sausage," Astrid recalled. "There was meat sausage and blood sausage and a few other kinds of sausage. The meat *korv* was salted down and later hung on long poles either in the pantry or the kitchen."

"The blood sausage was especially good," Nanny put in, "and we ate that up in a hurry!"

The old saying about using every bit of the pig but the squeal was certainly true. "We made *sylta* of the cooked head. The liver was either cooked or made into liver sausage or pate. But one part of the pig that was never eaten at Christmas was the ham. It was salted down along with much of the meat in a huge barrel. Some of the salted meat might be brought out at Christmas, but the ham was always saved until spring, even into the summer."

After the butchering came the baking.

"Mama would say, 'Now it's time to go get flour,'" Nanny remembered, "and off we went to the mill to get our grain ground. We baked *matbrod* (the regular dark mealtime bread), *smakakor* (little cookies) and *pepparkakor* (ginger cookies)."

It was almost Christmas now, and time to scrub the whole house from top to bottom. When it was shining clean and smelling of strong home-made soap, the new rag rugs were laid down, the ones their mother had been weaving all fall and winter on her noisy loom. (In earlier times small, snipped cedar twigs were strewn over the floor.)

But there was one chore left.

"The day before Christmas eve," smiled Astrid, "a big tub was set out near the stove and filled with water. One after another, each in our turn, we children hopped into the tub and got a good scrubbing.

"And when we woke up on Christmas Eve," continued Nanny, "we saw the beautiful new curtains that had been hung up during the night."

Both agreed that gifts were never important.

"It wasn't always that we were given gifts," Astrid recalled. "But if we were it was something practical, like mittens and stockings. Sometimes we wished that just once we would get something that wasn't so — so useful."

"But," added Nanny, "the best part about Christmas was, after all, all the good food."

An elderly Norwegian friend agreed that gifts were never an important part of Christmas.

"The special thing," she remembered, "was that we were all at home together. While my mother cooked rice pudding for Christmas Eve, my father read stories to us children. This is the thing I remember most."

One of the loveliest and most complete descriptions of Christmas in Sweden (and most of it would be true of Norway and Denmark as well) is in "Of Swedish Ways" by Lily Lorenzen. In that account she quotes a young American student who describes *julotta,* the early morning Christmas service in Skane, where he was visiting:

"I insisted on going to *julotta,* and as they had no car I walked the three miles to the nearest church, the kind of church I had always dreamed of worshipping in for *julotta* in Sweden. It was set on a high hill in a small village and with the lights from candles, the village Christmas tree lights and the candlelight from all the village houses, the scene was visible for miles around. It was quite fantastic — a Danish-type church, red tile roof, stepped front, and eight centuries old. The inside, lighted with candles, was decorated with evergreens and two large Christmas trees. *"Var hälsad, sköna morgunstund"* could never have had a more beautiful earthly setting. The minister himself was quite marvellous — well-padded with good Skane food, so that his heavy jowls made his bib pop up and down as he preached. His sermon on St. John's chapter on The Light was meaningful and presented in a personal, ordinary tone not always characteristic of Swedish pastors. As I walked home through the Minnesota-like woods and hills, the sun came up and I realized that it had been a long time since I had felt such peace and satisfaction."

Reprinted by permission of the publisher, Dillon Press, Minneapolis, MN., from Of Swedish Ways *by Lilly Lorenzen.*

By the Julian calendar, Christmas fell on January 6, 13 days later than our present Christmas. In times past — and to a certain extent today — the celebrating of Christmas went on through that whole time. The Church may, in fact, have had to take a hand in bringing the feasting and drinking to an end.

For the folklore and church lore accompanying the Norwegian calendar stick gives January 6 as the day on which ends the Christmas celebration proper. On St. Brictiva's Day, January 11, all the leftovers from the Christmas feasting were to be mixed together and eaten up, and all the Christmas ale was to be drunk up. Neighbors went from place to place helping with the "clean-up."

Finally, on January 13, the Twentieth Day of Christmas, the church bells pealed out a warning that the celebrating was over and it was time to get back to work.

This was the day the farmers and their hired hands were to begin chopping timber to add to the dwindling woodpile. The year had come full circle.

8.

Favored Foods

Good Scandinavian food is sheer pleasure. If it can be compared to the food of any other country, it would have to be to that of France's provincial cooking, depending as it does on good, simple ingredients, pleasing combinations of foods, a use of various sauces and an uncanny feel for using spices to give unique character.

But ask anyone who has a Scandinavian grandmother and he or she will insist, "I cook some of the same foods but try as I will I can't make mine taste like Grandma's did!"

Sometimes it's just memory playing tricks on us. Grandma's food is associated with Grandma's kitchen, the smells of soap and oatmeal cookies and fruit soup and clothes fresh off the line; the big wood range with a shiny rod along the front where snowballing grandkids could dry their wet mittens over the open oven door; freshly ground coffee coming to a foamy boil in a heavy aluminum coffee pot; a long coarse roller towel by the sink and embroidered flour-sack dish towels on a rack by the pantry door; crusty brown bread loaves, three to a deep black pan; a crocheted rag rug in front of the stove (if you peered closely you'd see scraps of your own old dresses in it), another by the sink, and faded ends of loom-woven rugs on which to wipe your feet outside the door. And best of all, a big round table to sit at any time of the day, especially when "forenoon coffee" or "afternoon lunch" came around.

But then again, maybe Grandma did things we've never learned to do.

Take sturdy dishes like meatballs and stew. Norwegian women never made stew *(lapskaus or labskaus)* of beef alone; always there would be diced pork in it, often salt pork for flavor. And where we settle for pepper and a bay leaf, she may have added a pinch of allspice and a dash of coriander. Swedish meat balls *(köttbollar* or *frikadellar),* too, should always be made with part pork.

Where my recipe for Swedish meatballs came from I've long forgotten, but 40 years ago I sent it to a bottled gas publication and won a whole $5 — and have used it ever since. In later years I've omitted the veal and will even settle for seasoned pork sausage, in which case I cut the seasonings in half. Here's the recipe:

1 pound ground beef
½ pound ground pork, unseasoned
½ pound ground veal
½ cup fine soda cracker crumbs
½ cup half and half
½ cup water
2 eggs
¼ cup chopped onion
1 teaspoon salt
¼ teaspoon pepper
¼ teaspoon nutmeg
8 or 10 whole allspice, crushed
Shortening or butter

Mix meats together. Soak crumbs in half and half. Stir in water, mix with meat. Fry onion lightly in about two teaspoons butter, add to the meat mixture along with the lightly beaten eggs. Add spices. Mix well, even kneading with your hands. Shape into balls smaller than a walnut, fry in a little butter or shortening over medium heat, browning on all sides. Add barely ¼ cup water to the pan, cover and let simmer on low heat 10 or 15 minutes. (Vivian Wilson of Geneva, Illinois, says margarine's fine for some things but she insists on butter for frying her Swedish meatballs.)

But again, there are touches Grandma never knew about. Mussling Rosenstand of Copenhagen adds grated zucchini to her *frikadellar* to keep them soft.

Since our two previous books, "Scandinavian Home Cooking" and "Notes From a Scandinavian Kitchen," dealt with so many of the foods our immigrant mothers and grandmothers cooked, we're not including many recipes here. Instead lets take a look at some of the "classics," those favorite foods that first and second-generation Scandinavian Americans think of as "old country."

And despite the chapter heading, we MUST deal with lutfisk. No other Scandinavian food (perhaps no other food, period!) has engendered such raves of ecstasy or such groans of horror.

The Wall Street Journal once sent a reporter to Minneapolis to cover the great lutfisk debate. There he found people who called lutfisk "one of the finest delicacies known to mankind" and others who countered, "If it's such a delicacy, how come most people only eat it once a year ?" Some called it Norwegian Jell-O. One woman remembered her first sight of lutfisk at the holiday table of her in-laws. "I thought, what did they do to the turkey?" One man said he'd never worked up the nerve to try it. Another insisted the Vikings sailed to American shores to get away from it.

But churches and fraternal groups still bring out crowds of people when they announce a pre-Christmas lutfisk dinner, most of them in Minnesota, North Dakota, Wisconsin and smaller Scandinavian enclaves like the Pacific Northwest. And if we need further proof that there are lutfisk lovers out there, figures show that a million and a half tons — yes, that's TONS! — of lutfisk are sold annually in the United States.

Swedes spell it "lutfisk" and pronounce it "loot-fisk." Norwegians put an "e" in the middle and pronounce it "loot-e-fisk." Although Danes eat it too, they don't get as fanatical about it as Swedes and Norwegians.

The Journal writer called it "a kind of tortured cod," which is as close as you can come to the truth. The Vikings may have carried on their journeys the dry cod that is the basis of the fish. The custom of eating it on Christmas Eve goes back to pre-Reformation days when fasting before Christmas was in order and one ate only fish on Christmas Eve.

Caught in icy northern waters, the cod is cut into large slabs and hung on wooden bars to dry in the cold wind. It dries hard as a board and could be kept for several years this way without spoiling. These board-like fish are crated and shipped, and while consumers in this country seldom see it at this stage, at least one of the fish stalls in Seattle's Pike Place Market has the dry fish hanging on a hook on the wall.

The soaking process is generally done by the fish importers, but in days past the housewife did it all. The fish is first soaked in water for several days, with the water changed each day. Then it is soaked in lye water, or packed in layers of lime with a soda solution poured over it. It is immersed in this solution for six days, a process that loosens the flesh. Finally, it is soaked in clear water another week, again with the water changed each day. By this time it has swelled to five times its dried bulk and only now is it ready to cook.

Even Julia Child, who lived in Norway for two years, says it can be tasty "if you give it a nice sauce." It should be cooked quickly and is often cooked in a cheesecloth bag to hold it together. Many now bake it in the oven, just to the point of flaking nicely. For the most part, Norwegians eat it with melted butter poured over it; Swedes prefer it with a cream sauce over it, sometimes flavored with home-made mustard. It was traditionally served on Christmas Eve with plain boiled potatoes and not much else, and with rice pudding and lingonberries for dessert. But today's lutefisk supper will likely have meatballs or baked ham along with it, together with a vegetable and some of the smorgasbord dishes. Today the fish can be bought in frozen chunks, ready to boil or pop into the microwave oven.

Perhaps the philosophy about lutfisk is best summed up by Charlene Olson of Mauston, Wisconsin. She says no one in her family likes it "but I cook a pound or two of it every Christmas to make the house smell right!"

Norwegians wouldn't think of eating lutfisk — or lutefisk — without *lefse*. Swedes are probably responsible for the jokes about lefse, saying you might as well butter your napkin and roll it up and eat it. But they're not above eating and enjoying the thin, chewy bread

~~~~~~

In the past the *seter* was a part of life in Norway. Many farmers who lived on lowlands around the fjords had temporary summer farms in pastures in the uplands. Many were in isolated areas in the high mountains. While the farmer and his sons tended the regular crops, the wife, daughters, younger children and in some cases maids would take the cattle up on the highlands for the summer. Here the cows grazed on grassy outcroppings. Living in cabins, the family would tend and milk the cows and make cheese for the winter. Today most Norwegian farmers feel it is too much trouble to move the cattle spring and fall, so the *seter* is used as a holiday home or a place to take summer guests. When they are used, refrigerated trucks now pick up the milk daily. And the cheese is made in factories.

~~~~~~

Like all good Scandinavian cooks whose cooking instructions are so frustrating to their daughters and granddaughters, Marie Asheim of Seattle doesn't use recipes for the old-time dishes. "Oh, I just take some of this and some of that and put it together," she smiles.

For the last 15 years, five days a week, Marie has gone to a Seattle institution for the retarded to serve as a "Volunteer Grandmother." But when she comes home she's happy to reminisce about the simple everyday cooking in her native Norway, where she grew up in Vats. When she came as a young woman to the Grand Forks area of North Dakota, there were so many Norwegians there that "it was almost as if I hadn't moved at all!" And their cooking and baking came with them.

Marie recalls that in her childhood home it was *potet kager,* potato cakes, rather than the thin-rolled lefse that were commonly eaten as we would eat bread.

"We'd cook the potatoes with the skins on, then put them through a *kvarn,* a grinder. We kids had to do that job, the kids always helped. Then we'd add a little salt and put in flour until it was easy to handle and then we'd knead it smooth. We'd pull off some of the dough and make balls, then pat them down with our hands to flatten and round them. You could stack them up until you were ready to bake them. We'd get a good, even fire in the big cook stove, kind of spread the fire out. Then we'd take off all the stove lids and lay a big iron sheet over the whole stove top and bake the cakes all over it."

These kept well but not as long as the *flatbrød,* which was stacked in piles in an upstairs room. This would keep for weeks. "Run up and get some bread," was a common reminder to the children.

"And we were always urged to eat bread," Marie remembers. "'You can't fill up without bread,' my mother used to tell us."

Their *flatbrød* was made from whole oats that had been ground at the local mill. "We just put water into the oat flour, nothing more. Then we kneaded it until it was very elastic and rolled it very thin, the thinner the better. Sometimes we put potatoes in it. Sometimes at dinner we'd put our potatoes and meat right on the *flatbrød* and eat it, or dip it in our soup."

The ground oats made good cookies, too, and *grøt,* or porridge. "It was a supper dish there. I was surprised to come to America and find people eating oatmeal for breakfast. My mother always said, 'I feel better when I have the *havre grøt* (oat porridge).' "

Marie remembers a special lefse made at her Vats home. It was made with mashed potatoes and rye flour, flour that had been ground very fine after the husk had been removed. (Now she uses wheat flour.) Rolled thin, this was baked for just a little while on the stove top, barely enough to stiffen it. Then, one after the other, the rounds of lefse were taken off and cooled completely.

"Now, this was made right after one of the cows had calved. The first milk that's milked after calving is very rich, very different. We took that milk and rubbed it on top of each lefse round, rubbing it around and around. It made kind of a shine, or gloss. Nowadays I beat up an egg with a little milk and put it on the same way."

At this point the lefse rounds were put back on the stove top, where the heat had cooled down somewhat. They were baked until the tops were dry, then turned and baked on the other side. They were stored away dry and when it came time to use them they were sprinkled with water and wrapped in a towel to soften them.

Buttermilk and soda went into the Hardanger lefse that Marie, like her mother in Norway, sometimes made. She agreed that "if there could be a recipe" to the way she makes it, it would be something like this:

2 cups buttermilk; 2 teaspoons soda; ½ teaspoon salt; ½ cup corn syrup. Flour enough to make it easy to roll out. This is not rolled as thin as other lefse. When it's partly rolled out, Marie goes over it with one of those notched rolling pins you'll find in Scandinavian gift stores.

Marie and her husband started farming in North Dakota in the middle of the Great Depression and the drought. She remembers the day her brother-in-law brought her a big bag of wool from sheep he had sheared.

"I didn't have a spinning wheel, so I went to Mrs. Ostlund, a neighbor, a truly helpful Norwegian lady. She had a spinning wheel. I spent one day with her and we carded and spun all that wool in a day so I could knit warm mittens for my husband. If I remember right, she even found time to make *raspkomla*."

At this point I realized why it is so hard to duplicate, from someone else's recipe, the foods that our Scandinavian mothers and grandmothers cooked. Truth is, the same food might be known by several names, and food of the same name might be prepared in several different ways, all depending on the cook, the area where she came from, and what she had found she liked best.

In past years a Norwegian woman was a good housewife if, at her son's wedding, she could produce some *flatbrød* she had baked for his christening. Aging, many thought, improved the flavor.

Marie agreed that *raspkomla* was what some Norwegians called *kropkaker*. Swedes called them *klub* or *palt*. We might call them potato dumplings.

"You ground raw potatoes and mixed a little flour in. Then you put some diced cooked pork in the center of a ball of this dough, and you cooked it in the broth where you'd cooked the meat, maybe a ham bone. Some use graham flour in it. Sometimes we'd add a little cooked and mashed potatoes to it; it seemed to make it softer."

It was Marie who reminded me of one of the classic niceties of Scandinavian desserts:

"We always used a fruit sauce on vanilla puddings and a vanilla sauce on fruit puddings."

The first crop the immigrant Scandinavian planted was potatoes. And the wives brought with them the know-how of using potatoes to extend almost everything, especially meat.

My favorite is potato sausage. Over the years I've altered the recipe a little, adding more meat in proportion to potatoes and more beef in proportion to pork. Stephen and Linda Ekstrand, who entertain their friends at a sausage-making open house every December, use a half-and-half potato-meat ratio and half pork and half beef. Linda adds ground allspice and has

experimented with garlic powder and marjoram and finds them both good.

But my sister, Sigrid Johnson of Minneapolis, says the classic old country recipe is the one Uncle John Nelson used in his butcher shop in Cokato, Minnesota, many years ago. The White Front Market had a white tile floor on the customer side and sawdust behind the counter and in the back room. Here you might find Uncle John and his longtime chubby helper, Allen Nelson (no relation), peeling washtubs full of potatoes for the sausage they made several times a week before Christmas.

That called for two parts of ground potatoes to one part of ground meat. The meat was always the very leanest pork; no beef was used. Salt (a teaspoon to a pound of mix) and pepper were the only spices. Here is a small recipe:

> 2½ pounds pork shoulder, as lean as possible
> 5 pounds potatoes, peeled and ground
> 1 medium onion, ground
> 6 level teaspoons salt
> 2 teaspoons freshly ground pepper

Mix thoroughly. If you don't have a sausage stuffer, use a wide-spout funnel, pressing mix loosely into sausage casings (available at many food specialty stores). Tie off sausage at intervals. To serve, bring to a boil in water to cover, then simmer for 45 minutes. Or bake at 350 degrees for 45 minutes.

Root vegetables of all kinds were staples before the days of the Mason jar and preserving. This popular smorgasbord dish makes use of two good keepers, beets and salted herring:

SILLSALAD (Herring Salad)

Clean, filet and skin one salted herring. Let the filets soak in plenty of cold water for about 12 hours. (Or use pickled herring.) Cut up the herring, two boiled potatoes, one peeled and cored apple, one small pickled cucumber and one onion, all in small cubes. Mix these with 3 or 4 cups of pickled beets. (Pickled beets are a Scandinavian home-canned staple but if you don't have them look for a can of Harvard beets at your supermarket.) Season with freshly-ground black pepper and a little of the pickle juice. Refrigerate for at least four hours. Garnish the salad, which you may either leave in the dish or mound on a platter, with sliced hard-boiled eggs. Serve with a small bowl of sour cream or unsweetened whipped cream. (Or these may be mixed with the salad immediately before serving.)

If you have access to fresh salmon, *gravad lax,* cured, marinated salmon, is a splendid buffet dish.

Filet about 3 pounds fresh salmon. Remove all small bones but do not skin. Rub the fish with a mixture of 4 tablespoons salt, 3 tablespoons crushed peppercorns. Place a very generous layer of fresh dill at the bottom of a shallow dish, then lay one salmon filet with the skin down. Cover with another generous layer of dill. Sprinkle with the remaining spice mixture. Place the other salmon filet on top, skinside upward and in such a way that the thin side rests on the thick side of the other layer. Cover with more dill. Place a light weight (not heavy enough to squeeze the juices out) on top. Refrigerate the salmon for one to two days. Turn it when half this time has passed. To serve, scrape off spices, cut in thin slices. Serve with cold mustard sauce: Mix 2 tablespoons prepared mustard, one tablespoon sugar and one tablespoon vinegar. Slowly add 6 tablespoons oil, stirring vigorously. This will thicken. Then add 6 tablespoons sour cream and plenty of finely chopped fresh dill.

Here is a basic recipe for Swedish pancakes, called *plättar,* or crepes:
½ cup heavy cream
1 cup milk
2 eggs
3 egg yolks
½ cup all-purpose flour
½ teaspoon salt
2 tablespoon melted butter

Beat eggs and egg yolks with ½ cup milk. Sift in flour and beat until smooth. Beat in remaining milk, cream, salt and melted butter. Let batter stand for at least an hour (till all bubbles disappear). In a lightly-greased and well heated (but not too hot) 6-inch crepe pan, drop 1½ to 2 tablespoons batter. These crepes are to be thin and browned on only one side. Continue making crepes, stirring batter now and then. It should not be necessary to grease the pan after the first time. Stack crepes between layers of paper toweling. At this point crepes may be used for various filled recipes or frozen for future use.

These may be used as dessert pancakes and are often served after the traditional Thursday meal of yellow pea soup with pork. If you can find a "plättpan," a Swedish iron skillet with 7 round sections (you'll also need a narrow spatula for this) you'll have small, round pancakes. You can also use a heavy skillet and make them about 3 inches in diameter. One tablespoon of batter should make one small pancake. Fry for a minute or two on each side. Serve at once with preserves, or stack on an ovenproof plate and keep warm in a 200-degree oven.

Almonds (mandel) are much used in Scandinavian recipes. For instance, the King's Almond Cepes (Kungen's Mandelcrepes):

Make the basic crepe batter but add ½ cup ground blanched almonds. Make crepes thin; brown on one side only. Fill with fresh or frozen berries, or with rhubarb cooked with sugar until soft. Heat in a 425° oven for 3-4 minutes till warm. Serve with ice-cold thick whipped cream flavored with rum or brandy to which caramel splinters have been added at the last minute.

Caramel: Melt ½ cup sugar in a heavy skillet until golden brown. Pour onto baking paper (buttered heavy brown paper, or waxed paper) and let cool. When hard, chop into fine pieces or splinters.

HANNA'S APPLE CAKE (Hannas Appelkaka)

¾ cup ground blanched almonds
1 teaspoon almond flavoring
3½ ounces butter
6 tablespoons sugar
½ lemon, juice and grated rind
2 egg yolks
3 egg whites
6-8 apples, precooked with sugar or raw, thinly sliced and sugared to taste.

Preheat overn to 400°. Place well-drained apples in a shallow buttered baking dish. Cream butter and sugar until light and fluffy. Gradually blend in egg yolks, almonds, lemon rind and juice. Beat egg whites until stiff but not dry. Carefully fold into almond batter. Spread batter over apples. Bake for 15 minutes until golden. Best warm.

They might top this with a sauce made by beating three egg yolks and three tablespoons of sugar to a light, fluffy mixture. To this add one cup heavy cream, whipped, and one teaspoon vanilla.

One dish which appears in almost every Swedish cookbook and in suggestions for Swedish smorgasbords is *Janssons frestelse* ("Jansson's Temptation"). Who Mr. Jansson was I've never been able to find out, but I trust he was a hefty Swede and this dish would surely have tempted him to go back for seconds and thirds!

Peel 8 medium-sized potatoes and cut into thin strips. Peel and thinly slice 2 yellow onions. Brown the potatoes and onions in a little butter. In a buttered baking dish alternate layers of potatoes and onions with layers of fileted anchovies (use one tin, about 125 grams). The top layer should be potatoes. Pour over this one cup of thick cream (into which you can mix any liquid from the anchovy tin, if you wish). Sprinkle bread crumbs on top and dot with butter. Bake at 350 to 375 degrees for about 40 minutes. Add another cup of cream and bake for another 10 minutes, until the potatoes are soft.

Here is Danish red cabbage fit for a king: In a large, heavy pan melt 3 tablespoons margarine. Add one medium head of red cabbage, shredded, and one medium onion, chopped. Cook for a few minutes, then add 3 tablespoons vinegar and 3 tablespoons water. Simmer for two hours. Add 4 red apples, unpeeled, chopped; a teaspoon salt, ½ teaspoon pepper, 2 tablespoons sugar. Simmer for another hour. Then add 3 tablespoons margarine, some red wine or a half glass of jelly (currant or raspberry) and a tablespoon of caraway or cumin seed. (A friend from Denmark cooks her cabbage in grape juice and uses lemon juice instead of vinegar. Some prefer wine vinegar.)

There is a certain anomaly in Scandinavian foods as we know them. On one hand there is the spare, frugal fare cooked by our immigrant grandmothers in the tradition of their homeland *stuga:* yellow pea soup, fish soup (from fish heads), brown breads, "farmer" cheese, porridges, pancakes, plain boiled potatoes. At the other end of the scale are the rich butter cookies and elegant coffee breads, flavored with everything from seeded raisins to marzipan to currant jellies. There are the handsome open-faced sandwiches and the almost-endless parade of both hot and cold dishes at the smorgasbord table.

Actually, for most of our forefathers and foremothers, life held a little of each. For even the poorest household ususally had a cow and some chickens, sources of all the magical milk, cream, butter, cheese and egg dishes the *husfru* cooked and baked. And for the immigrant settlers, a cow was one of the first purchases they made.

Cousin Nels Norbeck of Corvallis, Montana, remembering his early years in Saskatchewan, where he came from Sweden as a five-year old with his family in 1907, recalls their first cow:

"The day Rosa arrived on our farm was indeed a memorable one. Rosa, Swedish for Rose, was a gray-brown dappled milk cow. I can still see Dad coming along the trail leading her, followed by brother Hans. We kids were really excited, surrounding and stroking her sides. Finally I saw Mother coming down the back steps walking toward us. When she got to Rosa, she put one arm around her neck, leaned her cheek against it, and we saw tears running down her face. This we could not understand; it was such a wonderful and exciting event and here Mother was crying. We associated tears with sorrow. In after years we came to realize that those were not tears of sorrow but of joy. Rosa meant milk for her family, milk for butter and cheese, and milk for the enrichment of the bread and the goodies she made."

Milk and cream certainly starred in one of Norway's classic "folk dishes" — *rommegrøt.* "I won't say a Norwegian will kill for it," said one of my Norwegian friends, "but that gives you an idea."

Borghild Sande, 85, of Seattle grew up in Christiansund, where she learned to be a seamstress. But she remembers her grandparents' farm home, with lots of milk and cream cooling in big cans.

"Rommegrøt was always served when there was a baptism or a burial," says Borghild, "or when everyone in the neighborhood came together for a house-roofing or something like that."

Borghild still cooks it occasionally for Bjarne, her husband of 65 years. But every Midsummer she put on her apron and cooks it for up to 165 people when the Fremad Society holds its annual Midsummer celebration at

101

Denny Park Lutheran Church. Fremad is a Norwegian-language group that has been meeting at the church for over 50 years, and Borghild has cooked *rommegrøt* for them almost that long.

This year she and her helpers started with 10 gallons of whipping cream.

"The dairy won't sour the cream for us any more, but we were lucky to find a farm where they'll use a culture to sour the cream in those quantities. It has to be good and thick."

Borghild agreed to share a "small" recipe with us. This is the amount she uses when, also once a year, she cooks the cream-milk porridge for the bazaar of the Foss Home Auxiliary, serving "only 65 to 70."

Here she uses 2½ gallons of thick sour cream, 12 quarts of milk and 12 cups of flour. ("Though I don't know that I ever have a recipe!") The milk is heated and kept hot. In a heavy pot, boil the cream 20 or 25 minutes, until it begins to look buttery and yellow around the edges. Sift in the flour gradually while adding the hot milk. Stir constantly so it doesn't stick to the bottom. Soon the porridge will be thick and all the yellow butter will be floating on top. Skim off the butter into another pan. Add "a little salt and a little sugar." Borghild says that "usually the women taste it and tell me when it's just right."

Rommegrøt should not taste sweet. Bland, rich and creamy-smooth, it is served warm in soup dishes, with a little of the melted butter ladled back over it. Sugar and cinnamon are sprinkled on top.

What about the really small recipe for Bjarne?

"Oh," smiled Borghild, "I just use less of everything."

For almost every holiday there is a special food. When Terri Minteer, a staff writer on the Bremerton Sun, spent a year in Sweden, she began hearing about *semlor* long before Lent.

"But why can't I taste them now?" she wanted to know.

It was tradition, her friends explained, to eat *semlor* (plural of *semla*) on Shrove Tuesday, the last day before the former long fast of Lent. The

102

custom goes back to pre-Protestant days when it was necessary to eat up all the forbidden foods before the fasting began. However, the bakeries and konditori now are bringing them out at least a month before Shrove Tuesday. Everyone complains loudly about this breach of tradition — but they buy and eat them happily! Terri said they varied from bakery to bakery, but she liked best the ones her friend's mother made:

SWEDISH SEMLOR

Scald two-thirds cup milk, stir in 6 tablespoons butter or margarine and cool to lukewarm. Add one package dry or compressed yeast and let stand about 5 minutes. In a large bowl combine 3 cups flour, ¼ cup sugar, ¼ teaspoon salt, ½ teaspoon ground cinnamon and ½ teaspoon ground cardamom (optional). Add milk mixture and one egg. Beat well to make a soft dough. Knead dough on board covered with ¼ cup (or more as needed) flour until smooth and elastic (takes about 10 minutes). Place in a greased bowl, turn over to grease top. Cover and let rise double in bulk.

When doubled, stir dough vigorously to expel air bubbles. Divide dough into 10 equal pieces and form each into a smooth ball. Place on greased baking sheet about 2 inches apart, cover lightly and let rise till doubled. Bake in 400 degree oven for 15 minutes or until lightly browned. Cool. (Freeze, wrapped airtight, if made ahead.)

Whip 1 ½ cups cream and sweeten slightly with powdered sugar. Have ready one can almond paste (expensive, but one can makes 10 generous portions). Cut a thin slice off the top of each bun and save. Scoop a teaspoon or two of bread from the center of each bun and mix in a small bowl with crumbled almond paste and ½ cup whipped cream.

To assemble, fill each bun equally with almond paste mix, top generously with whipped cream and replace the slice of bun on each one like a lid. Dust with powdered sugar.

Eat out of hand or, better yet, serve in a bowl of steaming hot milk and eat with a spoon.

For some very different desserts here are two Icelandic recipes passed on to us by Joanne Jonsson. We're especially happy to include these, for space has prevented us from including background on Iceland and Finland, both of whom are "Nordic" countries.

BRUNHILDUR'S SKYR

Preheat oven to 275 to 300 degrees. Empty a half gallon buttermilk into metal container or ovenproof glass container. Place on middle shelf of preheated oven. Turn oven off and let sit until puddles form on top of buttermilk. Remove from oven and pour into a container covered with linen or cotton tea towel. Pour the buttermilk so that it rests on top of the cloth and the liquid can become separated from the solid. Let sit for a few hours (overnight is OK). Spoon the curd into the bowl of a food processor or mixer and beat, adding either half and half or milk until it is the consistency of yoghurt, either custardy or runny — your choice. Refrigerate. Serve with brown sugar and either half and half or milk. Also very good with blueberries sprinkled over the top.

VINARTERTA, AMMA'S FAVORITE

Cook and pit two pounds prunes. Put through food grinder or food processor. Add ½ cup prune liquid, one cup sugar and ½ teaspoon cardamom seeds, crushed. Cook till as thick as jam. Add one teaspoon vanilla (or whiskey, wine or rum). Set aside while you cream one cup butter with one cup sugar. Add 2 slightly beaten eggs and one teaspoon vanilla. Sift together 4 cups flour, 2 teaspoons baking powder, ½ teaspoon salt and add alternately with ¼ cup milk. Dough should be firm but not stiff. Chill. Divide into eight portions. Roll out each on a lightly floured board to fit an 8-inch pan. Turn cake pan upside down. Place rolled out dough on ungreased bottom of pan and trim the edges neatly. This recipe should yield at least 12 layers. Be sure to use the trimmings. Bake at 350 degrees about 10 minutes, until layers are just starting to brown. The layers should not be over ¼ inch thick.

Spread cooled filling on cooled layers. Press the finished *vinarterta* with the palm of the hand to make the many layers of cake blend with the filling. Wrap tightly in a dry cloth. Let stand at least overnight with a weight placed on top of the cake.

Whether one was rich or poor in the old days of Scandinavia, the custom was to eat plain fare for everyday but to be ready to serve very special things at festive times.

One of the many local histories published in Sweden in the last years is *"En Bok Om Ljungby"* ("A Book About Ljungby"), dealing with a parish in southern Sweden, near Falkenberg. A paragraph in that book sums this up poignantly:

"There are two characteristics found in all the Ljungby celebrations in times past — church ceremonies and an abundance of food.

"The Church's influence over holidays went hand in hand with the people's living faith in God. The food gave a festive air during those times when people often had a scarcity of food for everyday.

"Nourishment of the soul and body gave people the strength to live more abundantly, not only during the high holy holidays, but also during the long, gray everydays."

9.

The Great Emigration

A thousand years had passed since the men of the North sailed out in their sleek craft to leave a violent imprint on the Anglo-Saxon culture.

A thousand years, and again they struck out from the shores of Denmark, Sweden and Norway — yes, and Finland, too — into the Atlantic, into the unknown.

Most of us who think of the Scandinavian emigrants of the 1800s think in personal terms: the year that Grandpa came; the trunk that Great-Great Aunt Martina brought; town histories in the Midwest full of Olsons and Johnsons and Andersons, Jensens, Borgs and Moes.

But we can scarcely imagine the staggering numbers of people who packed themselves into the stinking holds of old ships, first the sailing vessels and later the crowded steamers, all with "America fever."

Sweden lost one million of its inhabitants to America— one-sixth of its population — in the hundred years between 1850 and 1950. Norway lost a greater percentage of her inhabitants to emigration than any other European country except Ireland. Most of these settled in Minnesota and North Dakota, though there were later emigrations to Australia, Canada and Argentina.

On the eve of the Civil War there were 72,000 Scandinavian immigrants in the United States. (Almost to a person they were anti-slavery and quick to enlist in the Northern cause.) The numbers swelled. The peak year for Scandinavian emigration was 1882, when over 29,000 Norwegians, 64,607 Swedes and 11,000 Danes came to the U.S. It is said that the shipping lines out of Goteborg were completely overwhelmed by all those wanting passage.

Denmark contributed less of its people than the other two nations. When the great economic crisis gripped Europe after 1870 (caused by huge amounts of cheap grain shipped from America, where the prairies had begun to be cultivated), Danish farmers turned to producing processed items like butter and bacon. But antiquated land distribution made this difficult, so many turned to the cities to become industrial laborers. Denmark had been industrialized earlier than either Sweden or Norway, so jobs were fairly plentiful. It was mainly those who missed the rural life and couldn't adjust to city living who eventually set out for the New World.

However, Danes had been leaving for America for many years, thanks in part to Mormon missionaries who were active in Denmark as early as 1848. By the time the Mormon Zion in Utah was closed in 1903, more than 16,000 Danes had settled there. Utah is full of Danish-sounding person and place names.

Actually, we would have to name as the first Scandinavian immigrants the Vinland voyagers of the 10th and 11th centuries, Biarni Heriulfson and Leif Eriksson, between 906 and 1003. Then there were Thorvald Eriksson and Thorfinn Karlsevni (1010-1013). The latter is said to have tried to settle a colony on what may have been Long Island, and a son was born here to his wife, Gudrid. But trouble with "savages" drove them away.

Anyone familiar with early American history remembers Peter Minuit as the first governor of New Amsterdam and the man who bought Manhattan Island from the Indians. But even before he reached the Delaware River, three Norwegians — two women and a man — had arrived with another Dutch group. Danes and Swedes later joined this same group and one of them became the first midwife in New Netherland.

When Minuit was eventually dismissed by the Dutch West Indies Company, he sailed to Sweden. There some wealthy Swedish and Dutch merchants agreed to form a company and establish a Swedish colony in America. Two of their ships reached the Delaware River in March of 1638 and several new settlements were built in "New Sweden." But disagreements developed over land and Peter Stuyvesant, with more troops than the Swedes, captured Fort Christina and took over the Swedish settlements.

But the influence of the Swedes came to be of help to William Penn in time, in terms of friendly relations with the Indians, an aversion to slavery, the first churches, mills, well-built log cabins and written laws.

What brought the later Scandinavians to America in such hordes?

Surely it was a combination of what they emigrated FROM and what they immigrated TO.

In Sweden in the early 1800s, most of the land was held by the nobility and the wealthy and it passed by inheritance to the eldest son. Even as in Viking times, younger sons must find other ways to keep up their position. Add to that the underpaid farm workers, their number increased by over-population; the crop failures of 1867-1869, and the harsh economic times in general, and it is easy to imagine the chill hopelessness that faced a man with a family to support or the youth contemplating his future.

Norway's population was increasing, too (sparked in the beginning, it is said, by the growing of potatoes as a generous food crop, a margin against famine). Lands there were subdivided until the holdings became too small to support those who farmed them.

(Reading Wilhelm Moberg's "The Emigrants" is a MUST! Never mind that you saw the film; it's the book that gives you the sense of what life was like when families made the decision to leave.)

There was much class distinction, ranging downward from nobility to government officials and clergy, landowners, shopkeepers, small farmers, renters and farm laborers. The right to vote depended on the amount of land one owned. At age 20, all men were expected to serve three months out of each of the next three years in severe military training camps.

The State Church came in for much bitter criticism. Pastors, paid by the state, enjoyed as much political prestige as spiritual standing in their own parishes. They often levied local taxes and kept most of it themselves. Many separatist groups like the Methodists and Baptists sprang up, but they were often forced to meet in secret. For anyone other than a State Church pastor, giving communion was considered a civil crime.

Is it any wonder that the stories and letters coming from America sent emigration fever to such a pitch?

"Chickens and ducks come raining down," promised a Swedish song of the time, "and roasted geese fly onto the table, a knife in the drumstick and a fork in the thigh!" The trees dripped with golden leaves. Beautiful young women smiled at one from every side. One had but to drop a plow in the land and the grain burst forth.

But even the plain truth was appealing. There was land to be had. There were jobs if a man wanted to work. Everyone was considered equal. A common laborer could shake the hand of a fine lady. No one asked you how you worshipped God. As soon as you were a citizen you could vote. There was timber for the cutting, game for the shooting and fish for the catching.

"America letters" were passed from one to another until they were in shreds. Soon pamphlets and books (like "The True Account of America" by Ole Rynning in Norway) fanned the flame.

Hundreds of ballads were composed, sung and sometimes printed in leaflets during the time of the mass emigration to America. Some were haunting expressions of sadness at leaving the childhood home. Others described the misery of the journey and the disillusionment of finding the New Land to be less than perfect. Still others were joyous, light-hearted, even ridiculous.

In a Swedish old people's home in West Newton, Massachusetts, Arne Menton heard someone sing "Pelle's Fantasy-Filled Yankee Doodle" in Swedish. He wrote it down and sent it to the Swedish newspaper, *Svea*. Knut Brodin published it in a Swedish collection of emigrant songs. Here is our translation, with a little freedom taken to make it fit the "Yankee Doodle" melody:

From Gothenburg to Boston
    town,
I find myself a-bursting
With all the luscious food I find
And grapes to slack my thirsting.

The meals are all three courses
    long
And silver is the platter.
My face grows greasy ear to ear,
But little does it matter.

The girls are angels and they
    speak
In English, e'en the humble.
Their shoes have only tiny heels
    —
They stand, but also tumble!

Their hair is all in ringlets here,
A hat on every daughter.
They live on pastries, every one,
Washed down with soda water.

The boys, we call 'em dudes, all
    smoke
And try to catch the lasses.
Their trouser legs are skinny-
    tight,
Their eyes have fancy glasses.

The animals are plentiful.
(Mosquitoes are the bummers!)
Of common folk, I'd say the
    most
Were Catholic newcomers.

Enormous swans live on for aye.
(I lie? I beg your pardon!)
I've watched them swimming on a
    lake
In Boston's Public Garden.

The town is huge and so are
    homes,
The size you must not doubt, sir!
The streets are paved with marble
    stone
And roofs pure gold throughout,
    sir.

And nowhere have I thrived so
    well —
'Tis heaven, very nearly!
Goodbye, live well, and don't
    forget
That Pelle loves you dearly.

Considering all this, the leave-taking should have been easy. Getting the passage money and enduring the voyage should have been the biggest difficulties. One emigrant, writing a family history when he was an old man, gives a straightforward, unemotional account:

"In the spring of 1852 my father, Magnus Jonason and family set out from Karlsham, Sweden, for Gotheborg in a small sail boat. The boat was manned by only two men and a boy of fourteen. It took seven days to reach our destination. At Gotheborg we had to wait three weeks for a sailing ship, the Ambrosius, carrying a cargo of iron to New York. Twelve men comprised the crew. The journey was made in seven weeks and two days, reaching New York on August 3, 1852."

But leaving was often anything but easy.

It wasn't just the strong, sentimental ties to family and friends and familiar places. It was not only their love of native land, a devotion that led them to write in their songs,

"There have I picked your flowers and gathered your
berries fair;
No other corner of all the earth can be as dear
as there."

But those who left often came under severe criticism — for any one of a number of reasons.

Even in the 1700s the kings realized that emigration meant a loss. After all, the country's population was part of the king's property, wasn't it? As early as 1753, Danish King Frederick V prohibited American sea captains from traveling around his country to spread propaganda about America.

~~~~~~

One of the "America letters" sent to friends in the 1870s makes the point that "neither in the matter of clothes nor in seats is distinction to be observed."

~~~~~~

Nor was the clergy happy, since they depended on the taxes of their parishioners for part of their living. In fairness, they may also have decried the motives that sent many to the New Land. In 1785 a pastor in Jutland issued a pamphlet which asked, "Has the Discovery of America Caused More Damage than Benefit to Humanity?" He answered his question in part:

"Not only is the basest mob, enriched with America's gold and silver, indulging in the worst dissipation and the wildest lustfulness, but lustfulness and extravagance has like a tidal wave flooded all the Christian world, yea, the entire globe."

There are those who would agree with Pastor Clausen today!

Others accused the *utvandrare* ("out-wanderer") of putting greed for wealth above love for country. If you will only stay, they insisted, things will get better.

110

Still others, caught up in the reform movements that were sweeping Europe and unsettling the whole social fabric, were even more bitter. Certainly the class system was wrong. Certainly people should be free to express themselves, to change their government, to worship as they pleased, to reform the great land holdings. But it would take strong, dedicated people to bring about these reforms. Setting out for America, they cried, was the coward's way out. Stay and fight!

But they went.

They went in sailing ships, some of them as old as 150 years. Well into the 1870s, after steamships were common, some sailing ships still carried emigrants to the New Land. With good weather, the trip from Gotheborg to New York could be made in six to seven weeks under sail. But those who signed for passage were told to bring food enough for 10 to 12 weeks and there were many voyages that stretched out that long. In 1846 Norwegian emigrants paid from $25 to $38 for a ticket.

Many of the ships had been converted to passenger carriers after a lifetime of hauling rough cargo. People were crammed into every corner of the dark, airless holds. Violent storms could send uper bunks crashing down on lower ones. Babies were born. Passengers died and the captain read the last rites of the Lutheran Church over the canvas-wrapped body just before it was lowered over the side. Seasickness could be excruciating. My mother, who came relatively late in the emigration, in 1899, sometimes —but not often — spoke of it. She recalled how she and a woman friend would take their quilts and roll up in the bone-chilling cold of the deck to get away from the stench of vomit and human bodies below.

Today many Scandinavians recall stories of the "networks" that helped the newcomer once he arrived. The first ones were the real adventurers; after that there was usually some relative or someone from the home area who would take them in for a week or two. They were the ones who knew where land was available or where jobs might be waiting.

Some were drawn to colonies founded on religious or idealistic tenets. There was Oleana in Pennsylvania, founded by Ole Bull, the Norwegian violinist, composer and patriot. There was Bishop Hill (Swedish) in Illinois and the Koshkonong settlement (Norwegian) in Dane County, Wisconsin. Each of these makes a fascinating study in itself.

Where there were railroads, they traveled inland on railroad cars, many of which were converted cattle and swine cars with plank benches around the sides. Others went by boat through the Great Lakes in quarters not much better.

The typical earliest settler in timbered areas might first throw up a shelter of light brush wood, thatching it with straw, branches, anything that would keep the rain out. By winter he might have excavated a dugout in a sidehill; while it sheltered the family from the terrible northern winter he would be able to fell trees and, in the spring, get a start on a small log cabin. He might break two acres of ground the first year and put in corn and potatoes. The following year, more potatoes and a little grain, and more breaking. By the third year he might be able to sell a little.

111

In the cities, the immigrant's first work was likely to be as a street cleaner or towman on a canal. My father, who came in 1890, worked on the Lake Erie docks and in steel mills and recalled the Swedes fighting with the Italians and Irish. It was not uncommon, he said, for a man to fall into the cauldron of molten steel around which they worked

The rich land around Chisago Lake in central Minnesota was a mecca for the earliest Swedes. The route to this area was by steamboat from St. Paul. The touching account of one family's journey was written many years ago by O. M. Linnell, who was a boy of 12 at the time, 1852. At the place where the boat docked, the cliffs of the St. Croix River rose like rock walls from 50 to 100 feet above the water. Behind them towered more rocky cliffs.

"The following morning at daybreak," wrote Linnell, "I found Mother weeping as she said, looking at the crags overhead, 'At last we have come to the land where one doesn't have to toil among the stones.' "

~~~~~~

The people of the North were never given to a great show of feelings. In "Growth of the Soil" Knut Hamsen paints a poignant picture of the father whose son is leaving home.

Isak stands by the window until his son has said the rest of his goodbyes. Then, quickly, peevishly, he grabs his son's hand and says, "Well, goodbye. There's the new horse getting loose." The father escapes to the yard where he himself had set the horse loose only a while before.

~~~~~~

It wasn't long before the culture of these new citizens began to root itself in this new soil. The first newspaper, *"Scandinavia"* (later *"Scandinavien"*), was started in New York in 1847, followed that same year by *"Nordlyset"* ("Northern Lights"). Others followed with names like *Hemlandet, RättaHemlandet, Decorah Posten, Den Norsk Americaner, Den Danske Pioneer, Ugeblad.* By 1874 there were no less than 10 Swedish newspapers in California alone!

Lutheran pastors arrived from all three Scandinavian countries and congregations sprang up quickly. Cultural societies were organized to foster homeland social customs.

Interestingly, these new arrivals were not necessarily welcoming to fellow immigrants. Records show that in 1886 many Scandinavians in Chicago joined "nativist" associations to oppose the immigration of new peoples from southern and eastern Europe.

Letters to the homeland during those years of "settling in" tell a conflicting story. On one hand, many followed trades which they had started in the old country, and prospered. Those who had gotten a start farming told that the corn was taller, taxes and rents were manageable, there was no begging, no fear of seizure, no class distinction.

On the other hand, there was much illness (usually described simply as "the fever."); not knowing the language held them back; they were homesick; they had expected better soil and less hard work; they lived too many to a room. And when someone got a little money ahead he struck out to buy land, leaving the penniless poor in the cities. One family wrote of living in a dugout until spring "when the snakes moved in."

It was hardest on the women. An article in the Atlantic Monthly in 1893 contrasts the life of an American farm family with that of one in Europe. There they lived in towns, their farm lands outside the city. They visited, gathered at the village well, church or school. Peddlers and priests made their rounds. In America it might be a mile or more to the nearest neighbor; the summers were hot and the winters cold; no trees or brooks broke the dreary landscape, and the family's life was lived in three or four rooms in a tarpaper house next to a sod barn with a straw roof.

Small wonder that many of them were anxious to put those years behind them.

Again and again, people of our generation say, "How I wish I had asked more questions when my parents — or my grandparents — were still living!"

What we should have done, perhaps, was to reassure them more that these were great, important accomplishments to talk of, that in becoming poor immigrants they had given gifts of immeasurable value to generations to come.

~~~~~~

Bernard Pearson of Foreston, Minnesota, has written an account of his parents' survival as immigrants from Sweden, "Einar and Lina." He tells of the morning Einar was to leave his home:

The table in the house was set with bowls and cups. On the two sides of the table were benches and on the ends there were chairs. These had all been made by Per Johanssen himself and were well built. He was an excellent wood craftsman, although most of his work was with wagon wheels and curved wood of all kinds. As they seated themselves at the table, there were Per, his wife Lovisa, and the following children: Ellen, Einar, Edla, Joe, David and Lydia. The four older daughters who were in America were Mathilda, Elizabeth, Lizzie and Anna.

113

There was a kettle hanging on a tripod in the spis (fireplace). After Per had asked the blessing, Lovisa went and got the kettle that contained their morning meal, gröt (porridge) made out of oatmeal. She ladled it out to each one.

Einar exclaimed, "Mamma, there are raisins in the gröt!"

"Yes," she said, "we tried to find something special today as we knew you would be leaving us." They all enjoyed the special treat and the conversation was happy and joyful. Einar reiterated his promise to send for them as soon as he was able.

Joe teased him, "I think he'll go over there and get married and forget all about us." They all laughed and Einar retorted, "Not me! But I will look for a girl for you!" Then he turned to Ellen.

~~~~~~

Although some of the Scandinavian emigrants were sons of nobility, most were those who would have fit this bit of advice which Benjamin Franklin gave the French in a 1794 pamphlet titled, "Information to Those who would Remove to America:"

"Much less is it advisable for a Person to go there who has no other Quality to recommend him than his birth. In Europe it has indeed its value, but it is a Commodity that cannot be carried to a worse Market than to that of America, where people do not enquire of a Stranger, Who is he? but What can he do?"

~~~~~~

"I still wish you would have gone with me. Now I have to bring back the money they sent for your passage."

"I'm not ready to go over there yet. If the folks and the rest go, I will go over then, too." That seemed to settle the matter and it wasn't brought up again.

After eating, Per took the Bible down from the shelf and read a chapter and then led them in prayer. He prayed for Einar, that God would keep His hand over him, both on the journey and in the future in the new land he had chosen.

After breakfast, Lydia had to go to school. The rest of the children had been excused to have opportunity to bid their brother farewell, but Lydia's teacher refused. She told her that if her brother was so dumb as to leave his homeland she shouldn't be allowed to enhance his going. Einar heard afterwards that Lydia had cried all day, which only brought more recriminations on her.

Reprinted by permission.

~~~~~~

10.

Tracing Your Ancestry

It was incredible. Here we were, four elderly children of Swedish immigrant, and none of us knew where our parents were born.

We knew their birth dates. We knew they were born in the province, or *lan*, of Halland in Sweden. We knew the years in which they emigrated to America. Vaguely we remembered place names they had mentioned. Church records in Minnesota listed only "Sweden" as birthplace.

Then, deep in a desk drawer of mementos, one of us found a memorial folder from the funeral of Aunt Anna, Father's sister. It listed her birthplace as "Alfshög, Sweden." At last we had a beginning. "Why I kept this all this time I don't know," said my sister.

From a list of archives in various areas in Sweden (this is available from the Swedish Embassy in your nearest large city), I found the one covering

Halland. I sent a $10 check, asking that they do as much research as they were able to for that amount. I enclosed all the information we had. But it was the parish name for Aunt Anna's birth that provided the key. Back came considerable information, going back as far as our great-grandparents.

If we want to know more, we can proceed in a number of ways. We could go to Sweden and search through the parish records of Ljungby Church. (Ljungby and Alfshög Churches lie only four miles apart, their tall spires easily visible from many of the rolling green hills in that area north of Falkenberg.) We could write to the archives and arrange for a researcher to do further digging in the records. (Although charged with record-keeping within their parishes, local pastors are under no obligation to help you do genealogy research, although most are as helpful as time will allow. Nor can the archivists do this during working hours, but staff members will, for a fee, do research on their own time.) Perhaps the simplest would be to contact the Genealogical Department of the Church of Latter Day Saints in Salt Lake City. The Department has extensive records on microfilm of all the Scandinavian countries. One may go there and use their facilities without charge or pay one of their genealogists to do the research. At this writing they have 11 genealogists accredited for Danish research, one for Finland, six for Norway and six for Sweden.

But archivists in all three Scandinavian countries emphasize that there are three important pieces of information everyone should have before starting to trace back the family tree there. They are 1) the original form of the name of your ancestor; 2) the date of birth, and 3) the name and location of the parish in which he or she was born. The last is particularly crucial — there are 2,000 parishes in Sweden alone and there are several instances of two or more with the same name.

But suppose you don't have these?

Begin by pursuing all the personal sources you can think of. Talk or write to Uncle Olaf and Aunt Gudrun and all the relatives you can think of, especially the elderly ones, even though they may only be distant cousins. Ask for any scrap of information they can remember about the person you're researching. Old family friends may have saved letters or pictures. Look in attics and basements, old trunks, old books — and encourage other relatives to do the same. Look for family letters, Bibles, books, journals, diaries, birth and marriage records, obituaries, announcements, emigration documents, family histories. If you have relatives in Scandinavia, even though from a different branch of the family, they may be able to shed some new light.

If you still haven't come up with what you need, go on to other sources.

If you should happen to know the name of the ship on which your ancestor arrived and the approximate date when he came, and if you know the port of entry, you can write the National Archives, Washington, D.C., for information. Manifests of all persons arriving after 1820 are microfilmed there. They will also copy an individual manifest for a fixed fee.

Census records may help. The 1850 census was the first Federal Census to give the birthplace of the person enumerated. If you know where your ancestor lived in those years after arriving, this is an excellent source. You can consult the records in the National Archives in Washington, D.C., or have parts of them copied for you for a fixed price.

Unfortunately, naturalization records are not in any central depository but scattered in many courts throughout the country. But if you know when and where your ancestor received his citizenship, those records will give you information on birthplace, date of arrival in America and sometimes even the name of the ship on which he came.

Death certificates are found in local city halls and county courthouses and, in some states, in the state capitol. These often give birthplace and date and next of kin.

Military records, also in the National Archives, land records and church records can be helpful. A microfilm project is underway in the U.S., sponsored by the Emigrant Institute in Vaxjo, Sweden, which eventually will cover all immigrant Swedish churches and list information on all those from Sweden who affiliated with them. Copies of those already processed are available at the Lutheran Theological Seminary Archives in Chicago as well as at the Emigrant Institute in Vaxjo and the Emigrant Register in Karlstad, Sweden.

Many books and directories about Norwegian immigrants have been published by local historical societies and others. Many of these may be researched in the Rolvaag Library of St. Olaf College, Northfield, Minnesota. The Vesterheim Genealogical Center is a splendid clearing house for this type of information. To learn about membership in the Center and subscription to its periodical, "Norwegian Tracks," write to the Norwegian-American Museum, 502 West Water Street, Decorah, Iowa 52101. Enclose a stamped, self-addressed envelope.

The Sons of Norway, 1455 West Lake Street, Minneapolis, Minnesota 55408, can provide information to help you start on your research. Again, enclose stamped envelope for reply.

In Canada, you may make inquiries about passenger arrival lists from 1865 on from the Public Archives of Canada, 395 Wellington Street, Ottawa, K1A ON3.

More detailed information is available in booklet form from each of the three Scandinavian countries. Contact the embassy or trade office for each in your nearest large city.

Suppose that through one or more of these avenues you've found what you were looking for. Let's say it's your grandfather, and you now know his full name and date of birth, also the name and location of the parish in which he was born. Now you want to know what other family he had, where his people came from and what other relatives you may have that you didn't know about.

It's much easier to trace backward than to bring a family tree up to the present. The latter will take a lot of digging and corresponding on your part. But tracing back has its limits, too; in none of the countries are you likely to get back further than the middle of the 17th century, although some noble lineage was recorded before that time.

Each of the three Scandinavian countries has local archives in which the older records have been deposited. In most cases, the oldest records are in the archives and the more recent ones in the parish churches.

The Danish provincial archives have the census forms from 1787 on, the draft register going back to 1788 and parish records from 1814 on. (Actually, some parish records go back to 1660, but fires have destroyed many rectories through the years and records prior to 1814, when they began keeping them in duplicate, are incomplete.) Many parish records between 1815 and 1874 note who left or arrived in the parish, in addition to births, marriages, confirmations and deaths. To learn which of the five provincial archives you should address your inquiry to, write to Danes Worldwide Archives, 2 Konvalvej, DK 9000 Alborg, Denmark.

In Norway, the seven regional archives contain all records from before 1900 (in some cases 1950). To learn which one serves the parish you are interested in, write The National Archives in Norway, Folke Bernadotte vei 21, Postboks 10 Kringsja, Oslo 8.

If you visit Norway, you may study all the documents in the archives and the staff will, within reason, help and advise you. Here, too, later records will be found with the parish pastor. Good information about farming families in Norway is often found in the rural chronicles called *bygdebøker*. A *bygd* is a country settlement that forms a topographical and, usually, administrative unit. However, most of these publications concentrate on the farms' owners and especially those who may also have been civil servants or in some other way members of the "upper class." There will be little information about renters or farm workers.

Sweden has the largest number of regional archives of the three countries. Even a few of the cities have been given the right to establish their own archives and handle the records of the churches and courts within their jurisdiction. The National Swedish Record Office will forward your request to the proper one. The address is: Fack, Fyrverkarbacken 13-17, S-100 26 Stockholm. If the information you're looking for is more than 100 years old, you will find it either in the regional or national archives. However, about 40 parishes, mainly in Dalarna, have been allowed to keep all their records.

If the records you seek are in one of those parishes, or if the information lies within the past 100 years, you'll find answers to many of your questions in the records. For one thing, there are the very interesting *husförhörslängder*. These were set up as a kind of report sheet for the pastor as he made his visits through the parish. Here he noted how his people were faring physically and spiritually, their occupations, departures and arrivals, educational status, character traits. He also listed others who boarded in the household— aged parents, servants, cobblers, tailors, retired military people and poorhouse inmates, who were often farmed out in the community. Some of these reports go back as far as the 1620s.

If you're going to do research yourself in the Scandinavian countries, you should be aware of a few difficulties.

One is that of name changes. As one Swedish historian puts it, "Thousands of Swedes (during the emigration) changed their names as easily as they changed their shirts." In the next chapter, we'll talk more about names. But you must be aware that in one generation the name may be Andersson, in the one before that Petersson and in the one before that Olafsson. And there could be a half dozen variations of each.

Another problem in Norway is the old Danish script used in most parish records. And in that portion of Denmark bordering on Germany many records are written in German.

"In fact," says B.A. Borgesen, a Scandinavian researcher for the Genealogical Department of the Mormon Church, "as a Dane I can travel from Copenhagen in the east to the west coast and find myself a total stranger inasmuch as the old population can cut me off language-wise if they start speaking 'westjydsk.' "

Which brings us to the services of this department of the Mormon Church — and they are extensive.

The Genealogical Department Library in Salt Lake City, Utah, has over 155,000 books, a million rolls of microfilm (40,000 rolls a year being added) and 300 film readers, all for use within the library. Assistance is provided and genealogical advice is available at no charge. The library does not provide actual research services, but has available a large number of accredited genealogists who specialize in various nationalities.

According to Borgesen, the Danish collection includes microfilm copies of Danish parish registers from the time they began (sometime in the mid-1600s but generally early 1700s) to about 1914; census records for 1771-1911; probate records from the 1600s to early 1900s, and some family histories and genealogies. For records of more recent date one must go to the archives in Denmark or the local parishes. Records less than 30 years old are not accessible to genealogical researchers without special permission, Borgesen explained.

The microfilm copiesof Norwegian parish records begin with about 1689 and early 1700s and continue through the 1800s. There are none from years later than 1900; rights-of-privacy laws have not permitted records to be filmed after this time. There are also census, probate and military records and some family histories.

For Sweden, the library has microfilm copies of vital records from the time they began (about 1689) to 1897. They also have census records, the Household Examination Rolls about which we talked earlier, probate records, tax lists and some family histories.

To contact the library about these services or about getting help from an accredited genealogist, write Genealogical Department, The Church of Jesus Christ of Latter Day Saints, 50 East North Temple Street, Salt Lake City, Utah 84150.

Is family research really worth all the effort it takes?

I think it all depends on what you're looking for. In no way will our self-worth be enhanced by anything we find in musty parish records in another land.

But you will find yourself reaching back across the generations to a specific name, a specific place, even a place that you might one day visit.

Too, your search could open up an interest in a whole era of European history whose excitement you missed when you studied it in school. Use your imagination and think what it must have been like for your great-great grandfather to live in Bergen when Ole Bull had started the Bergen Theatre and Henrik Ibsen was managing it. Who knows, you may find a far distant relative who was a struggling artist in Copenhagen when Hans Christian Andersen was a struggling poet! Wouldn't that be exciting to that grandchild who is so adept at drawing? Scandinavian literature will come alive to you when you realize that certain of your ancestors likely read it when it first came out, probably in magazine form.

And the search itself will grip you as if you were unraveling a mystery or solving a puzzle.

And if the *husförhörslängder* states that your great, great-grandfather was "indolent and given to tippling a bit," you can always comfort yourself with the fact that things have improved mightily through the generations.

120

11.

What's In
a Name?

More than you think!

Tracing one's ancestry must be much easier in countries where the family surname doesn't change with every generation!

That's what most Scandinavian names did from earliest times until the 1700s and many well into the 1800s.

At first there were no surnames. Who needed them? Everyone on the gård knew everyone else. They all knew, for instance, that Peter was the son of old Elias by the bridge *(Bro Elias)*. When Peter had a son and gave him the name of Knut, he was known as Knut, Peter's son. Peter's daughter, Anna, was known as Anna, Peter's *dotter*, to distinguish here from Anna, Lars' *dotter*. When Knut married and had a son, he became Oskar, Knut's son.

This custom of Christian names only along with a patronymic identification was dominant in Sweden, especially in rural areas, until late in the 1800s. By then it had evolved into a written surname: Peter Eliasson and Anna Eliasdotter. Peter's children would have been Knut Petersson and Lovisa Petersdotter; Knut's children, Oskar Knutsson and Olivia Knutsdotter. But by the end of the 1800s the patronymic identification of each generation had ended and surnames became permanent in the family.

The same was generally true in Denmark and Norway, except that the suffix there was *sen* and the double "s," which has also been dropped by many Swedes, was not used.

Nils William Olsson, editor and publisher of the Quarterly Swedish American Genealogist, has done some interesting research on Swedish names, and we are indebted to him for most of the information in this chapter. Olsson notes that members of the aristocracy were the first to adopt family names as far back as the 15th and 16th centuries. By the 17th century the clergy was adopting family names. Later in that century citizens in towns and villages began to change from names like "Thomas the smith" or "Sven the tailor" to fixed family names.

How some of these names came about makes fascinating history. The nobles usually took a name from the symbol inscribed on their coat of arms. Thus *Ture Jonsson Tre Roser,* a Swedish political leader who died in 1532, was so named because of the three roses inscribed on his family crest. One of the oldest families of nobility had an escutcheon on which the upper half was gold, the lower blue. The family came to be known as *Natt och Dag* ("Night and Day"), a name carried by the family to this day.

At first the clergy Latinized their own names. Thus Andersson became Andri, Petersson became Petri, etc. Soon, however, they began to adopt new names, using the Latin equivalent of Swedish words. Some of them were pretentious indeed, like the hero in Ludvig Holberg's comedy who sought to impress his home villagers by naming himself after the Swedish word *berg* but changing it to the Latin *Montanus*. A young Danish student, instead of adopting a name from his home village of Broby ("Bridge Town"), translated it to Latin — *ponto* (bridge) and *oppidanus* (town) and called himself Pontoppidan.

Other members of the clergy or students studying for the vocation chose to add the Latin *ius* to a Swedish name — Darelius, Nobelius, Topelius. Others added *aeus,* still others *ander* as in Bolander, Elander, Kylloander, Tholander, Thelander, Mellander. The name was passed on down and often succeeding generations who were not clergy would lop off the Latin ending; thus Nobelius was shortened to Nobel.

As time went on and the population increased, people were encouraged to adopt non-patronymic names to lessen confusion in parish and military records. But when the ordinary man, the artisan or shopkeeper or farm worker, came to picking a name, he had no coat of arms to which to go.

Nor could he infringe on the clergy's Latinizing style.

The Danes and Norwegians usually solved it by taking the name of their farm or dwelling. (To this day Norwegian houses have names; no matter what the name of the families that live there through the years, the house name always remains the same.) At first the clergyman, who was responsible for keeping parish statistics, would write, for example, *"Olaf Olesen i Laingen"* ("Olaf Olesen in (the farm of) Laingen"). Many clergymen omitted the *"i"* and wrote simply "Olaf O. Laingen." Consequently many Norwegians dropped the patronymic entirely and used the name of the farm, home or possibly village from which they came.

The Swedes and Finns went a different route. They created their names from the nature around them. It may have been an unconscious effort to borrow from the nobility — not their names, which was illegal, but the same technique. But instead of words with reference to military exploits, they chose the vocabulary of the peaceful Swedish countryside.

For many years they were mainly two-syllable names. Now more are taking three-syllable names.

Here are a few of the more common nature-names taken from the topography of the countryside:

Aker - field, arable land	*Hall* - a rock formation
Bäck - rivulet, brook	*Holme* - island
Berg - mountain	*Lund* - a grove
Dal (old form was *Dahl*) - valley	*Mark* - land, ground
Fall - a clearing in the forest	*Skog* - forest
Flod - river	*Strand* - shore
Fors - rapids	*Sund* - narrows

Many of these can stand alone as names. But the common practice was to combine two of them to form a name. Take the combinations with *Berg* alone: Engberg, Brantberg, Bergdahl, Dahlberg, Fallberg, Flodberg, Forsberg, Hallberg, Holmberg, Kjellberg, Landberg, Lundberg, Skogsberg, Stromberg, Bergstrom, Sundberg, Bergstrand, Berglund and more.

Taking names from the names of trees was popular:

Ahl - elder	*En* - juniper
Alm - elm	*Fur* - pine
Asp - aspen	*Gran* - fir
Bjork - birch	*Lind* - linden
Ek - oak	*Ronn* - mountain ash

Flowers and other parts of plants were also incorporated into names:

Blad - leaf	*Blom* - flower, bloom
Gren - bough or branch	*Ljung* - heather
Kvist (anglicized to *quist*) - twig	*Ros* - rose

123

Less common but also used were names of fruits, birds, animals, fish, points of the compass, the word *ny,* (new), military words and some foreign names.

But in spite of all this imaginative naming, hundreds of thousands of Swedes still clung to the "son" names — as witnessed by the Minneapolis phone directory!

This created a problem, both in Sweden and in this country. Often there would be two, three and even more people of the same name in a small community. Then other means had to be found to identify them.

In the community where I grew up there were two John Chelgrens. One was tall, the other short. No one knew them as anything but *Longe John* and *Lille John* — "Long John" and "Little John."

"Little John's" daughter, Hannah Eastlund, and his grandsons, Don and Conrad Grundahl, recalled some of the by-names that identified old-time Swedes around Cokato, Minnesota:

Sota ("Soot") Swenson. He cleaned chimneys.

Söndags ("Sunday's") Nils. It may have been the fact that he was a very pious church member.

Dräng Nils. His father was a hired man on a farm.

Kari vi broa. Carrie lived by a bridge.

Sme ("Smith") Anderson, the local blacksmith.

Tepp Gustav och Tepp Edwin, two Peterson brothers who came from Teppa in Sweden.

Skåning Olson, who came from Skane in Sweden.

Tilda pa mitten ("Tilda in the middle"). She lived at a crossroads, "in the middle of" four roads.

Henry Hanson, associate professor of history and social sciences at Northern Virginia Community College, writes in the Swedish American Genealogist about some of the by-names he remembers from a small Connecticut town before World War II, at a time when some of the immigrants were still living. He recalls one Albert Johnson:

"Albert Johnson was a short man, so he became known as *Pojken Johnson* ('The Boy Johnson'). His wife was known as *Pojkens käring* ('The Boy's Wife'). His son was known as *Pojkens pojk* ('The Boy's Boy'). And his grandson in turn was given the by-name of *Pojkens pojkes pojk* ('The Boy's Boy's Boy')."

The names were seldom forgotten.

Professor Hanson remembers one young woman who was given the unflattering name of *Rova* ("the Buttocks").

"It seems," he writes, "that as a young child she attended Sunday school in the local Lutheran Church. Her father complained that the sexton had done such a poor job of keeping the toilet facilities in the church clean that his wife had to *tvätta Annas rova* ('wash Anna's backside') when she came home from Sunday school. The name stuck, and when this person came, as a 60-year old, to visit my 90-year old mother, my mother referred to a visit to her by *Rova*."

12.

Explore Further

*"Yes, thousands of years hence they
will come flying on wings of steam
through the air and over the ocean.
The 'electro-magnetic wire' will
have 'telegraphed the size of the
aerial caravan' as young Americans
travel to see Europe."*

*Hans Christian Andersen,
1805-1875*

The Danish poet and tale-teller Hans Christian Andersen once remarked
that "to travel is to live; then life grows rich and vibrant. Man renews
himself, not as the pelican from his own blood, but from the great world
around him."

In this last section, we invite you to renew your own sense of identity with your Scandinavian past. Maybe you'll do it as you travel to the land of your forefathers, or maybe in travels to other places. Maybe you'll find yourself enriching your knowledge — or that of others — right in your own home community. These are only ideas to get you started on exploration. Your own curiosity, your own sense of cherishing the past that has gone into your present — this will, we hope, lead you into exploring more.

Explore!
World of Museums

"Runes shalt thou find
and letters bearing meaning
letters most mighty
which the Great Counselor
colored."
- Havamal

To some people the very word "museum" invokes a picture of boredom. To some tour group members it recalls memories of "Hurry!" The bus stops, tourists pour into a museum for a half hour, pour back out, pile into the bus and head for the next stop.

Museums are meant to be absorbed, slowly, leisurely, (and in comfortable shoes). They are to be savored. But the contents should hold real appeal for the person visiting; no one should be dragged through exhibits in which he or she has absolutely no interest.

For this reason alone, Scandinavia is a traveler's delight for there are museums dedicated to a whole smorgasbord of interests. Are you a castle buff? Denmark alone has over 300 castles and manor houses; there are whole tours dedicated to castles alone. Do the Middle Ages interest you? The Museum of National Antiquities in Stockholm is the central museum in Sweden for prehistory and the Middle Ages. Would you have liked to be a Viking sailor? Lose yourself in the Ship Museum in Bygdoy, near Oslo, for a day. There are art museums, like the outstanding Edvard Munch Museum in Oslo and the art collection (including his own fine works) which Prince Eugen assembled in his Stockholm home, Waldemarsudde, and which he gave, along with the home, to the Swedish people.

Restored early dwellings are to be found in Skansen and the Nordic Museum in Stockholm, the Open Air Museum in Lyngby near Copenhagen, and at Bygdoy near Oslo. Many smaller communities have similar collections and other charming museums, like the Sykkylven Museum of Natural History in Norway's fjord country. The 60-some museums in Copenhagen and its environs include exhibits of theatrical

126

history, farm implements, tram cars, medical science, coaches and harnesses, the Dutch influence, musical instruments, monastery ruins — and more. And for a moving experience, visit the *Hjemmefront Museum,* the Resistance Museum, at the Askerhus Fortress in Oslo and in pictures and displays sense the courage of Norwegian resistance during the German occupation.

But you need not travel to Scandinavia to find museums that put you in touch with your heritage. There are only three in the United States, but they are located on each of the coasts and in the center of the country so are quite accessible.

The oldest is the American Swedish Historical Museum in Philadelphia. Located in a building modeled after a 17th century Swedish manor house, the Museum stands on land settled by Swedes prior to William Penn's arrival in Pennsylvania. There are 14 galleries containing materials that interpret over 300 years of Swedish influence on American life. Included are rare examples of early glass, textiles, paintings, drawings and etchings. Seasonal observances, films, lectures, special exhibits and symposia, together with a 12,000-volume library make it a rich cultural and research center.

In Decorah, Iowa, is Vesterheim, The Norwegian-American Museum focusing on early immigrant America. The word *vesterheim* is one used by the immigrants from Norway in referring to their home in the west as opposed to their homeland in Europe. The Museum was founded by Luther College in 1877 and incorporated as a separate institution in 1964. A tour of its exhibits is a tour through history, with home furnishings, costumes, old tools, church furnishings, toys and other items that were part of life in Norway and in the early settler's home. There are several historic buildings in the complex.

Relatively new on the scene is the Nordic Heritage Museum in Seattle, Washington. Organized to "deepen our knowledge of the Pacific Northwest settlers who came from the five Nordic countries," the Museum is beginning to build a collection that will date from the 18th century. Although it already has an interesting collection, the emphasis of this Museum is on its being a Nordic cultural center, a "live" museum where traveling exhibits, plays, concerts, lectures, film series and classes are held throughout the year.

And while The American Swedish Institute in Minneapolis is not strictly a museum, its beautiful setting is a museum in itself and it has a number of interesting old collections. But it is primarily a cultural center, encouraging and promoting the Swedish cultural heritage through lectures, concerts, exhibits and educational programs. All of these institutions welcome memberships.

Have you ever thought you might establish a Scandinavian museum in your own community?

In terms of money and time — even of purpose — such a project may not be justified in your area. But a museum is not necessarily a PLACE with

OBJECTS in it. It can be an event, any effort that helps interpret the past. It can be as simple as an afternoon coffee hour in your home with a display of your grandmother's *hardanger* embroidery or as ambitious as a week-long demonstration of pioneer Scandinavian farming and homemaking crafts in your town mall. A town museum in Cokato, Minnesota, observed a year of "Scandinavia Today" with several exhibits and demonstrations of Scandinavian crafts, most of them by local residents. A shop in your town might be willing to provide space for an exhibit and sale of Swedish glass or Danish cheese or Norwegian knitted wear. In conjunction with it, find people willing to demonstrate embroidery, rosemaling, weaving, carving or other crafts. Have someone on hand to explain and interpret the exhibits.

You'll find lots of interested spectators and probably more willing participants than you might think. Most important is that you recognize the urgency of recording and re-living past history while those who were involved in it are still with us.

In 1979 Carla Wulfsberg carried out an excellent project in Seattle. Many of her ideas could be adapted to a greater or lesser degree in other communities.

Titled, "When Washington Was a Wilderness (1900-1930): Our Nordic Heritage of the Twentieth Century," the project was a "celebration of living legacies."

"We have by no means collected, written or produced a complete history of the Nordic people in Washington," wrote Wulfberg in her introduction to the project booklet. "That will have to come. But if we must name our own purpose, it might be this: to celebrate the history surrounding each of us, and acknowledge the individual's experience of it."

Interviews with 56 Danish, Finnish, Icelandic, Norwegian and Swedish immigrants to Northwestern Washington were taped. Family photographs and documents were copied. The project grew to include discussions with a panel of scholars, a slide and tape show, an information booklet, exhibits, tours of historic buildings, films and workshops in preservation techniques and concerts of Scandinavian music.

Funding came from the local Arts Commission and the state Commission for the Humanities. (In other projects like this, funding might come from private businesses, Scandinavian organizations or fund-raising connected with the project itself.) Churches, senior citizen centers, a museum, a theater and an antique store provided space for nine consecutive days of events, some daytime, some evening.

How many times we think, on reading the obituary of some elderly resident of the community, "Oh, how much history he could have shared with us!" Of course he could have — if someone had asked. Or, maybe they asked, but no one recorded it to share with others.

One of the biggest services you could do your community in terms of preserving the part played by Scandinavians in its past is to tape interviews with some of the older people. Have them tell you stories their parents and grandparents used to tell them. Ask about their arrival in America, or that

Fishing at Frederiksborg

of their parents. Get family histories. Do they remember funny stories, riddles, games, jokes, proverbs in their Scandinavian tongue? Do they remember sermons or religious experiences that had a profound effect? Songs and hymns?

Where do you find these people?

The American Folklife Center suggests that you start with your own family and friends. They may furnish you with leads. Check with pastors of local churches, ethnic shops (such as Scandinavian food stores), Scandinavian lodges and senior citizen groups. Don't overlook nursing homes and retirement homes. In one of them I met Inger, who remembers her childhood in Frederikstad, where her father was captain of a passenger boat to Oslo. Again and again she was allowed to hop aboard the boat, spend the day in Oslo and travel home again with her father. She told me much about the "network" of relatives and friends who helped newcomers when they first arrived in America.

~~~~~~

Vivian Mackey of Seattle, who has traced her own family tree and helped others through a "Scandinavian Interest Group" in the local Genealogical Society, suggests family tapes as wedding presents. As a wedding gift for young members of her family, she tapes the marriage service. Then on the other side of the tape she transcribes segments of family tapes she has made over the years. Through this, children yet unborn will be able to hear their great, great-grandfather reading "The Star Spangled Banner" or hear a great, great, great-aunt tell how things were done when she was a child, or hear voices at a long-past family reunion chatting, singing, laughing, reminiscing.

~~~~~~

A friend who does a lot of interviewing of this kind says, "At first they all insist, 'Oh, I can't remember much, I have nothing interesting to tell.'

"But ask them, 'Do you remember how your grandmother looked? What kind of aprons did she wear? What was on her parlor table? How did the house smell?' And the first thing you know, they are right back in that place and time!" Sometimes the presence of a third person helps; one may jog the other's memory. Again, it may inhibit some of them.

The American Folklife Center, Washington, D.C., will give you good advice on conducting interviews. Here are some of their suggestions on the use of a tape recorder:

1) Respect the person's wishes. Always request permission to use the recorder and tell how the recording will be used (for archives, a program, educational, etc.)

2) A relaxed and comfortable interview is the most enjoyable and productive. It might be good at the beginning to offer to play back the recording for approval and comment.

3) Look directly at the person and respond to statements in an encouraging way. You are a part of a conversation so don't be preoccupied with the machine.

4) Don't be afraid to have your own comments and questions on the tape. They place the documentation in a proper context.

5) The Center recommends 60-minute cassettes since longer cassettes use tapes that increase the likelihood of scratching and tearing.

6) Try to set the microphone as close to the subject as possible or use a clip-on mike.

7) Label your tapes immediately. Include name of speaker, name of interviewer, date and address of taping and nature of topic (story, handcraft, family history, etc.)

8) Store tapes in a dry place away from electronic or magnetic equipment.

The material you collect is valuable in many ways. While it may have much to do with your personal interest, the material can also be valuable to others. Community centers and organizations might like a copy. Museums often receive, present and preserve materials having to do with the region and its cultural heritage. Schools and colleges would be interested in knowing about historical information you may collect. Local newspapers welcome stories on community history, especially if you have good black and white photos to accompany them. Be sure your subject gives permission for the material to be used in this way.

Tape recorded interviews are very special, says Carla, "because the sound of a family member's voice, their way of telling a story, and perhaps their unusual dialect or way of speaking is wonderful to have as a family legacy."

As helps to you, she recommends two books, "Underfoot" by David Weitzman (Scribner); and "Oral History Primer" by Gary L. Shumway (inquire of California State University, Fullerton, California.)

(Museums: The American Swedish Historical Foundation and Museum, 1900 Pattison Avenue, Philadelphia, Pa., 19145; Vesterheim, The Norwegian-American Museum, Decorah, Iowa 52101; The Nordic Heritage Museum, 3014 Northwest 67th Street, Seattle, Washington; The American Swedish Institute, 2600 Park Avenue, Minneapolis, Minnesota 55407.)

Explore!
Before Columbus

*"Runes of victory shalt thou know
if thou wilt have the victory,
and cut them on thy sword-hilt,
some on the hilt-rings,
some on the plates of the handle,
and twice name the name of Tyr."*
- Sigrdrifumal

In the year 986 Eirikr Thorvaldsson settled down on his farm, Brattahlid, on the sloping shores of West Greenland. Here he would greet his friends, who knew him best as Eirikr the Red, and they would spin tales of their voyages between Norway, Iceland and Greenland. Of the rest of the past Erik (as we know him) spoke little. But the dark memories must have haunted him, the killing for which he was first exiled from Norway, and the second murder, committed in a frenzy of anger, which had exiled him from Iceland and sent him first to settle this lonely coast.

Erik held to the old gods. But he could not prevent his wife Thjohildr from turning to the new religion, and in the year 1001 or 1002 it was she who built the first Christian church in the western hemisphere.

Little did Erik dream that for the next 500 years this icy and turbulent sea would carry fellow Norse adventurers up and down the coast of a new land. How could he guess that they would tramp the forests, harvest wild-growing crops, attempt settlements, encounter strange races of people and penetrate deep into the interior by inland waterways? Not only would his own son Leif add to the knowledge of this new land expanse, but there would be many more.

Their audacity and their adventures would make the voyage of Christopher Columbus pale indeed, and would prove for all time that Columbus discovered nothing that was not already known.

The accounts of those voyages to the coast of North America are a "must" reading for anyone interested in the early Scandinavians. They have come to us through Iceland's ancient *Eiriks saga rauda* and the *Graenlendinga saga,* but also through archaeological findings. Painstaking detective work on these as well as on old maps, scraps of written history, studies of climate, folk tales handed down and language discrepancies have raised claims and counter claims. Disputes still rage over interpretations of words, maps, navigation routes and relics. But more and more it is accepted that Leif Eriksson's discovery of America's mainland was not an isolated incident. It was only the beginning, and history as we've known it will have to be rewritten.

That these explorers sprang originally from Icelandic families is not strange. Iceland was settled largely by dissident chieftans from the *viks* of Norway when Harold Fairhair set himself up as the first Norwegian king. They brought with them their boat-building acumen, their navigating skills and above all the thirst for adventure and the daring that had made them chiefs in the first place.

One of the first explorers was Bjarni Herjulfsson, who around 905 was sailing from Iceland to Greenland when he was blown far south, then west, off his course. He found land, but when he realized it could not be Greenland he worked his way back. He encountered land twice again, finally reaching Greenland.

This account excited Erik's son Leif. Leif either bought or leased Bjarni's ship and in 1001 or 1002, keeping the experienced crew, he sailed Bjarni's course in reverse. He found land in three places and named the sites Helluland (Slatestoneland), Markland (Timberland) and Vinland.

The location of Helluland is more or less accepted as Baffin Island. Markland may have been Nova Scotia. The location of Vinland has been placed at anywhere from Ungava Bay in Laborador to Cape Cod and Rhode Island. More archaeological finds will have to be made before a location can be determined with certainty.

Much of the debate about Vinland, which was explored and even settled for a time by Norsemen, centers on the meaning of the word *vin.*

Did it mean "grapes?" Early historian Adam of Bremen states categorically that it meant they found grapes for wine. Others say the Norsemen had no knowledge of making wine. But some point out that Karlsefni, a later settler in Vinland, had with him Tyrkir, a German. Tyrkir not only found the vines but is quoted as saying, "I was born where vines and grapes are no rarity."

Then there is this argument, that if there had been grapes, Vinland would have been an important colony for now-Christianized Greenland; apparently they made no use of the resource for in 1237 the Greenlanders were still being chastised by Rome for using beer in the sacrament. Some scholars contend that *vin* referred to "good land," specifically good pasture land, for both Leif and the later Karlsefni had cattle aboard their ships.

Wherever it was, Vinland was the destination for an amazing number of voyages from the West Settlement of Greenland in the next 15 years. Between 1004 and 1006 Leif's brother Thorvaldr sailed to Vinland, found himself a fjord-like setting for a homestead, but was killed by natives, called *skraelings* or *skrellings*. In 1008 another brother tried to reach Vinland but failed, and died. Leif took in his widow and befriended her. When Thorfinn Karlsefni reached Greenland from Iceland, he met and married Gudridr and together they sailed to Vinland in an attempt to colonize it. Their son Snorri was born there. But by 1015 they had returned to Iceland and remained there.

In 1014 began a chilling episode. Freydis, Leif's cold, self-seeking sister, wanted to make her own expedition to Vinland. She and her weak-willed husband joined two Icelandic brothers, Helgi and Finnbogi, in an expedition of two ships. Once in Vinland, Freydis convinced her husband that the brothers had insulted her. She forced him and his crewmen to go aboard the other ship at night, where they axed the sleeping brothers and their crew. And when Freyda's crewmen refused to kill the five women aboard the ship, Freyda took the axe and dispatched the women herself.

By 1266 the Norsemen of the West Settlement of Greenland had made contact with the Eskimos, who seem to have been migrating eastward at the time. There are indications that trading between them led to more cultural crossing-over — the adoption of the kayak, for example, and the Eskimo house-building method. Gradually these Norsemen, too, may have grown nomadic. It may have been that the "Little Ice Age" disrupted their farming. But it may also have been that hunting caribou for meat and skins came to be an easier way of life than survival farming in a near-Arctic climate.

At any rate, by 1342 the colony in Western Greenland had ceased to exist. Father Ivar Bardson, a Norse Greenlander sent by the Iceland Lawspeaker to investigate, found a large church and some wild cattle and sheep, nothing more. There were no settlers, no *skrellings*.

Had they died out as the climate grew colder? They had been there as late as 1327, for that year the Christian settlers in Greenland sent the Pope's representatives 250 walrus tusks as a tithe. Some believe these settlers reached Greenland during a warming cycle but as the climate changed they either died of malnutrition or, in the case of some, were assimilated into the Eskimo tribes. Skeletons from the area show they had rickets and dwarf-like bodies, signs of continual starvation. Earlier Viking graves were at least six feet deep; those of the last Norse inhabitants were barely deep enough to cover the coffin, indicating that the ground never thawed more than a few inches even during the summer.

Still, studies of the Dorset Eskimo, the Skraelings, the Thule Culture, the Tunnits and the so-called "Blond Eskimos" provide some fascinating speculation. The Newfoundland Museum in St. Johns, Newfoundland, has many artifacts from these peoples.

But proof of the Norsemen's penetration of North America is by no means limited to the eastern seaboard. All kinds of Nordic finds have been documented from the Hudson Bay watershed to the Mississippi River watershed. In fact, some researchers believe there was a genetic remnant of the Norsemen in the Mandan Indians of North Dakota, a tribe wiped out by smallpox in the mid-1800s. They were described as having an obvious mix of Caucasian blood and a European influence in their folk tales.

By far the most exciting find, one that indicates that the Norsemen traveled over Hudson Bay country and possibly over water ways in what is now the Red River Valley, is the stone found by a Minnesota farmer near the small town of Kensington in 1898.

Olaf Ohman was digging out a tree stump when he unearthed a flat stone almost three feet long with runic characters on it. Eventually the runes came to be translated:

"(We are) 8 Goths (Swedes) and 22 Norwegians on (an) exploration journey from Vinland round about the west. We had camp by (a lake with) 2 Skerries one day's journey north from this stone. We were (out) and fished one day. After we came home (we) found ten of our men with blood and dead. AVM (Ave Virgo Maria) save us from evil.

"(We) have ten men by the sea to look after our ships 14 days journey from this island. (In the) year (of our Lord) 1362."

(Translation is by Hjalmar R. Holand; words in parenthesis were added by him for clarity.)

The controversy that has swirled around this stone for soon a century originally centered on its rejection by the University of Oslo, where it was called an example of "the irresponsible trickery that characterizes the American people." (Remember, this came at a time when the Norwegian scholarly community greatly resented the emigration of so many of its people to America.)

Frustrated by the derision that followed, Ohman finally dumped the stone face down on his granary floor and left it there for nine years. Holand encountered it while he was writing a history of Norwegian settlements in Minnesota and he would spend the next 50 years of his life researching Nordic exploration of this continent and writing books to prove that the Kensington stone had been chiseled by Norsemen.

Evidence of ancient waterways, the age of the tree in whose roots the stone was trapped, the weathering of the inscription, the integrity of the farmer, the discovery of mooring stones, camp sites and 14th century implements in the upper midwest, historical evidence of an expedition — Holand used them all.

He theorized that a party of Norwegians and Swedes reached these parts in 1362, having left a boat-guard of ten men on the shores of Hudson's Bay. Twenty men pushed on as far as Lake Cormorant, near the present town of Kensington, where 10 were killed by Indians. And the Kensington Stone became "the oldest native document of American history." (Holand)

But not everyone agreed with his findings. There is a "deathbed confession" by a man who said he helped Olaf Ohmann chisel the characters on the stone. In a 1958 book, Erik Wahlgren charges that the inscription is not medieval but appropriate to "Minnesota dialect," and that the stone is "a clever and understandable hoax."

Even Theodore C. Blegen, Dean Emeritus of the Graduate School of the University of Minnesota and a veteran Minnesota historian, published a book in 1968 pooh-poohing the stone and speculating on the "hoaxers." Scandinavian laymen at the turn of the century, he stated, understood and could translate runes.

But more recent conclusions lean toward the premise that Norsemen in the 1300s actually did reach Minnesota and the Dakotas. In 1981 Paul H. Chapman used navigational studies of the Vinland voyages not only to pinpoint Vinland's location but also the lands visited by the sons of Erik the Red and the route that led a later search party into the interior. ($1,000 was offered anyone who could find a factual error in Chapman's earlier book on the Norse discoverers; there were no takers, but one Ivy League publisher warned Chapman he was not likely to have such a book published by a university press because "it is too far from previously accepted concepts.")

Robert A. Hall, Jr., Professor Emeritus of Cornell University, in 1982 declared at the beginning of a scholarly essay that he had "no axe to grind" in the debate over the stone. But, concentrating chiefly on the inscription's characters, he delved into the linguistic and philosophical considerations. The essay was published in book form. The title? "The Kensington Rune-Stone Is Genuine."

In Alexandria, Minnesota, where the stone rests in an attractive museum, the community accepts the charges and counter-charges with good humor. "It keeps us on the map," said one. But one resident, a former teacher and a specialist in medieval history, has been quietly studying runes since 1952.

"There is no way," says Margaret Leuthner, "that uneducated settlers could have inscribed that message with its hidden meanings — it had to have been conceived by a medieval mind and in order to interpret it you have to think as they did."

Leuthner herself has located six smaller stones whose chiseled symbols indicate that Vikings died in Minnesota and North Dakota from the early 1100s to the mid-1300s.

What were they doing then, these voyagers so far from home?

Holand contended they were on a "holy mission."

In 1353 King Magnus of Norway, a zealous churchman bolstered by tithes granted him by the Pope, was preparing to march into Russia to compel the Greek Orthodox Catholics to accept the Church of Rome. But the plague had spread such death in Russia that Magnus turned his attention to Greenland instead. He dispatched Sir Paul Knutson with a well-manned expedition to undergird the Christian faith of the colony. It seems likely the group did not return to Norway until 1363 or 1364.

Where did they spend the intervening years?

Holand theorized that, finding the Western Settlement abandoned, Knutson pushed on to the west, seeking any shores to which the remnant of the colony may have dispersed.

No less than four widely diverse sources prior to 1555 agree that the expedition reached Hudson's Bay in or about 1360 and here divided into two parts. We can only guess whether they found any remnants of the dispersed Greenlanders, those among whom Sir Paul was to establish Christianity because, in the words of King Magnus, "we will not let it perish in our day."

Explore!

Speaking the Language

> *"Like men they journeyed for gold*
> *and in the east they fed the eagle,*
> *in the south they died, in Serkland."*
>
> Stone at Gripsholm,
> Södermanland

Wouldn't it be fun to be bilingual — especially if one of the languages happened to be your ancestral tongue?

Learning Swedish, Norwegian or Danish is not nearly as difficult as you might think. A Teutonic language, Scandinavian has developed along lines parallel with English. In Viking times Norsemen and Englishmen could understand each other fairly easily. Many English words are either identical or similar to Danish, Swedish or Norwegian words meaning the same thing. If you've studied German, it will be even easier for you. And if as a child you learned enough of one of those tongues to speak to your grandfather in his native language, you'll be amazed how quickly words and usages come back.

You needn't live near a university or cultural center to learn. If you can find a recent arrival from the country you're interested in, or someone who has kept in touch through frequent trips to the "old country," encourage him or her to start a conversation class. Work with simple books at the same time. Reading children's stories in the original Scandinavian is lots of fun for there are nuances of meaning, especially the humorous ones, that can never be translated quite literally.

But maybe you're one of those who has traveled in Norway and has found you could make yourself understood in one part of the country but not in another? Or you discovered that some Norwegians can't understand each other and have to turn to English in order to communicate? Or you're asking if it's really true that schools in Norway have to teach TWO Norwegian languages?

Ed Egerdahl of Seattle, who is both a student and teacher of Norwegian and who travels there often, tells of his experience.

"I had been visiting relatives in northern Norway and came down to Oslo to visit others there. In a very serious conversation, I was telling them that one of the relatives up north had to have a complicated operation on her jaw. Suddenly they all burst out laughing. That's when I found out the word for 'jaw' is the same as the word for 'flapper' in the south — she was going to have her 'flapper' operated on!"

The Norwegian language is definitely in a state of flux. It is a fascinating story, but it can be frustrating to anyone trying to sort it out.

But it's easy to understand how it came about. The Norwegians are a proud, independent, stubborn, self-reliant people who are extremely proud of their "ethnic Norseness." But for almost 500 years they were under the rule of others. Before that, they had suffered terribly from the Black Death. They had been fleeced by the German Hanseatic League which operated from Bergen (and left a smattering of low German in the dialect). A Swedish king took the throne in 1319 and by the end of that century Norway was under Danish rule, continuing until 1814. That gave way to only a little more autonomy under Swedish rule. And Norway had barely gained its independence in 1905 when World War I turned Europe upside down. On the heels of that came a worldwide depression, then Hitler, World War II and the German occupation.

That this mountainous land with so many of its people isolated from one another survived at all as a nation is a tribute to the resilience of its people. Small wonder that Norway had other concerns than establishing a national language.

Since it had no national center while under Danish rule, Norway had no choice but to accept Danish as the written idiom. It was during the years under Denmark that the printing press came into being. Textbooks all came from Copenhagen. The University was in Copenhagen. Pastors preached to their congregations in Danish, a factor in the alienation of so many Norwegians from the Church, even though they are nominally members.

But the rural areas ignored Danish and among themselves clung to their local dialects. In the southeast a common speech evolved and spread. But even this had differences. For solemn occasions Danish was spoken but with Norwegian pronunciation and many Norwegian words. The people spoke a local vernacular. In between was a sort of mixed language with a little of each. People would pick and choose, speaking as they wished.

Then in the late 1800s, authors like Ivar Aasen created a new-old literary language, discarding foreign words (including Danish and Swedish) and going back to the ancient Norse as much as possible. Sparked by strong patriotic movements, this *landsmal* ("language of the land") was used in many of the books published at that time.

But no one spoke it. They went on speaking their dialects or the *riksmal* ("language of the nation"), the language of the southeast.

After years of discussion, legislation and more argument, Parliament in the 1950s declared *bokmal* ("book language"), based on *riksmal,* and *nynorsk* ("New Norwegian"), based on *landsmal,* BOTH to be acceptable

138

national languages. Consequently both must be taught in the schools in this sense: in Oslo and its environs, where people speak *bokmal*, the children must learn *nynorsk;* and in the more remote areas, where people speak their local dialects, the children must learn *bokmal.*

The attitude seems to be, "Let's go ahead and use both languages, but use whatever we like of each." Even news broadcasts mix the dialects.

Because of this mix of "modern" Norwegian, Norwegian-Americans who came to America as children and who go back remembering their childhood Norwegian are in for a surprise.

"My father, who came to America when he was six, went to visit in Norway at age 56," recalled Egerdahl. "He remembered a lot of his Norwegian but people there found it stilted and strange. Even his 90-year old aunt spoke a different, more modern Norwegian."

The Norwegian Parliament also tried to initiate a new counting system, more like that of the English, using "twenty-one, twenty-two, etc." instead of "one and twenty, two and twenty, etc." But change comes hard. Scarcely anyone paid any attention. Egerdahl remembers a letter in an Oslo newspaper in which the writer excoriated the public for being so slow to adopt the new system of "twenty-one, twenty-two, etc."

"After all," the writer fumed in conclusion, "it has been five and twenty years since that ordinance was passed!"

Actually, you can still hear the pure old Norse language spoken in almost the same way it was in the eighth century and written in an even more similar form — in Iceland.

The Icelandic language is very close to the old Norse. When the early Vikings gradually separated into eastern and western Scandinavia, the language in the two sections also began to change gradually. The language of the Norwegians became West Norse, that of the Swedes and Danes East Norse. Since the settlers in Iceland were Norwegians they spoke the West Norse and still speak it today, though present day Iceland has a much larger vocabulary and different pronunciations.

And everyone in Iceland understands one another. There are no confusing dialects as in Norway and, to a lesser degree, Sweden and Denmark. Iceland is a small country. Most of its people have always intermingled with others throughout the country. Some farmers were nomads. Great numbers went down to the sea each year for the fishing. The Althing, the governmental body, brought people together from all over the country once a year. Few people left, fewer still have immigrated into Iceland.

As a result, anyone in Iceland who reads (and it is a highly literate country) is able to read its 12th century literature in the language in which it was written. So loyal and dedicated are they to that language that in 1918 a group of purists founded an organization to purge the language of Latin-based and other foreign words. And many words have never found their way into the language in the first place. For example, tuberculosis is still called *berklaveiki,* the "barking sickness."

Explore!

The Norwegians in Hawaii

"It is hard to know where your shoes pinch when they are not on your feet."
- Norwegian proverb

Norwegians in Hawaii? Yes, and some Swedes, too, and under some very strange circumstances.

It was toward the end of the 1800s. America's Civil War had been both a bane and a blessing to the Hawaiian Islands. When the war all but ruined the New England whaling fleet (some ships were converted to merchant ships, others were sunk to block Charleston harbor), the islands' already-dwindling trade with the whalers ground to a halt. But as the American South lost its sugar industry, plantation owners in Hawaii geared up to make fortunes off cane. By 1866 there were 32 plantations and mill companies in the islands as compared with 12 in 1860.

But the Chinese coolies were proving to be unreliable cane workers, always wanting to be tradesmen or house coolies instead. The Japanese were worse, causing trouble between the planters and the government. The Portugese and Filipinos suited the planters somewhat better.

But on a 900-acre plantation on the island of Kuaui, Christian L'Orange, a Norwegian owner, had an idea. His partner, Waldemar Knutson, son of Norway's titular head of government under Swedish rule, refused to take him seriously.

"Import Norwegians to work in the cane fields?" Even the Hawaiian Board of Immigration scoffed. Hard workers, yes, but they'd never be able to stand the climate.

But when the demand for laborers became desperate enough, L'Orange was allowed to sail to Norway and recruit a shipload of Scandinavians.

He brought back not one shipload, but two — 600 Norwegians with a smattering of Swedes among them. They had set sail from Drammen, families and single men and women. The first load arrived in Maalaea Bay, Maui, on February 18, 1881, the other three months later, both after a grueling half-year journey of heavy storms and high seas. Twenty-four people had died. Seven babies had been born, including one to a couple whose three other children had died during the journey.

The Norwegians had not been completely taken in by L'Orange's glowing promises, and it had taken considerable persuasion to get them to sign three year contracts. About a third were assigned to Oahu and Kauai and apparently adapted to their new life for little more was heard from them.

~~~~~~

Danish law requires that every time a tree is cut another must be planted. The Forestry Act of 1805 was enacted at a time when the forests had been reduced to only four percent of the country's land area and they feared there would not be enough native lumber for houses and ships' hulls.

~~~~~~

But for those assigned to Maui and Hawaii, their worst fears were realized. True, the agents had told the truth about the climate, the sea, the beauty. But their new homes turned out to be isolated camps in wind and dust-swept cane fields, a clutter of shacks and sheds. Married couples got a room ten feet square, separated from a line of similar rooms by head-high partitions. There was a common water spigot somewhere on the grounds.

Planting, weeding, irrigating, cutting, bundling and loading the cane was all done by hand. The early-season harrowing and cultivating went on in clouds of dust. The fine shag of the cane leaves irritated their skin as they stripped leaves from the stalks. Soon they found out that while the contracts they had signed in Norwegian provided for food for all the wives, the contracts signed by the planters in English provided food only for the wives who worked. The lunas, or overseers, were not above using whips to enforce orders. And there was much complaining about the food. German laborers, too, had been imported; they missed their beer and bratwurst, the Norwegians demanded butter and potatoes.

The Norwegians were by no means the first ones to complain. But they had an advantage: they were literate. They wrote letters. They wrote to newspapers in Honolulu, in Norway and Sweden, in America. One letter to the Hawaiian Gazette in Honolulu compared their examinations in Honolulu to the fairs at home, "where cattle are being sold, only they did not know who of us was the fattest; thus we were sold one here, another there; those that were not disposed of went to another island, there they got a master over them......."

Newspapers took up the cause. They were the first ones to use the term, "slave labor," and the workers immediately picked it up. (Actually, the contract they had signed for three years specified that a laborer had to work 10 hours a day in the fields or 12 hours in a mill, 26 days a month, for which a man was to be paid $12.50, a woman $8. They were to receive board, lodging and medical care, such as it was. However, mysterious deductions brought the pay down to $9 a month for men and $4.50 for women.) In Scandinavia newspapers and public meetings demanded that investigators, backed up by warships, be sent to the islands.

Finally, only ten months after the arrival in Honolulu of the second ship of Norwegians, the Swedish king sent a diplomatic representative to look into the matter. It took six months from the time of his appointment to his arrival and during that time plantation owners had hurriedly corrected many of the abuses. But on the day career diplomat Anton Grip arrived in Hilo, he found that 50 of the 60 Norwegians on one plantation had gone on strike, and since the Hilo jail was too small to hold them a number were being shipped to a Honolulu jail.

In the end the planters agreed to pay board and room for the nonworking wives. Money was substituted for food allowances for those who wished it. Skilled workers were moved to jobs that better suited their abilities and their pay increased accordingly. An inspector general was appointed by the government of Hawaii to look out for the rights of contract workers.

Most of the Scandinavians eventually returned home. But a number of them stayed and their descendants have settled into the life of the islands and have become successful in a number of professions.

(University Press of Hawaii has considerable information on these years as do books in the Lahaina, Maui, library, among others. Ingrid and Leonard Clairmont, a Swedish-American couple who settled in Hawaii in 1968, have written a moving historical novel about those Norwegians. "Blood in the Furrows" is published by Exposition Press, New York.)

Explore!
The Biggest
Viking Festivals

*"The fields are harvested and empty,
And here we are home with the last load.
We raked the field lightly, in treasured tradition,
So the poor and the birds shall have their share.
The harvest is in, let us feast now and dance!"*

- Danish harvest song

If not the biggest, they are surely the most colorful Viking festivals in the world! Not in Drammen, not in Bergen, nor Goteborg, nor Copenhagen. Not even in Minneapolis!

One is a nine-day extravaganza in Largs, 30 miles from Glascow, Scotland, the only Scandinavian festival on the Scottish mainland.

The other is in Lerwick in the Shetland Islands. It lasts only one day — but what a day!

Largs is a seaside resort city on the Firth of Clyde that attracts hundreds of thousands of visitors each year. It is also the site of a famous battle in 1263 between the Scots and the Norwegians, a battle that marked the end of Viking rule in mainland Scotland and the Western Isles. In that year aging King Haakon IV mustered at least 120 war galleys (some say almost 200) to try to protect Norway's weakest possessions — the Orkneys, Hebrides and Isle of Man. But the Scots were ready. The defeat of a Viking party that attempted to land at Largs forced Haakon to call off the campaign. Three years later the Hebrides and Man were sold to the Scottish crown. It is to commemorate that battle that the Largs Viking Festival takes place. It's in its fourth year and plans are to hold it each September.

The Festival, in a setting of sea and mountains, pays tribute to the Age of the Vikings through exhibitions, lectures, competitions and spectacular battle reenactments. There are demonstrations of Norwegian culture, skills and talent as well as Norwegian singers, dancers and entertainers, making it a truly international affair. Iceland and Shetland are also represented. There are Scottish bagpipes and Norwegian folk songs, a teenage Viking disco, the Norse Pageant Society, water sports, sailing races, art exhibits and historical walks.

143

Largs, on Scotland's west coast, is easily reached by public or private transportation. International airports at Glascow and Prestwick are close by, with coach connections to Largs. There are frequent rail connections with Glasgow. For more information write Largs Information Centre, The Promenade, Largs KA30 8DG, Scotland.

Unlike the fairly young festival at Largs, the "Up Helly A' " of Lerwick in the Shetland Islands (more commonly called Shetland) has been going on for 100 years on the last Tuesday in January.

In Shetlandic, "the helly" still means "the weekend," referring to the holy day of Sunday. So "helly" may at one time have referred to the religious element in the old pagan Yule celebration which marked the return of the sun in midwinter. Just as in the 16th century "Uphaliday" was the end of holiday time on January 6, so "Up-Helly-A' " was formerly the end of the Yule festivities. (Shetland seems at some time to have doubled the length of the Yule feasting.)

All of this started during the Norse occupation of Shetland, which lasted from Viking times until 1469. In that year King Christian I of Norway needed a dowry for the marriage of his daughter Margaret to the heir to the Scottish throne. Christian was already 34 years in arrears in his payments to redeem the Hebrides and the Isle of Man, and needed to produce 60,000 guilder in cash. He mortgaged the Orkneys to Scotland for 50,000 of these and at the time of the wedding mortgaged Shetland for 8,000 of the remaining 10,000 guilder owed. (After giving up Shetland for only 8,000 guilders, Christian five years later borrowed three times that much from the German Hanseatic League for a journey to Rome.)

The fact that Norwegian language and culture stayed alive in Shetland for several centuries after that probably explains why Up-Helly A' is such a rousing, rollicking festival in the middle of a wet, cold winter.

Far back in the celebration, blazing tar barrels towed through the streets of Lerwick were the main attraction. After big bonfires, "guizers" would put on entertainments, going from house to house, where doors would be open for feasting and dancing. (At least they were allowed to dance on the stone floors of the kitchens, sparing carpets and furniture from tar.)

Gradually, a magnificent torchlight procession, now with about 850 participants, took form. The guizers are grouped in squads, about 50 squads in all. Each squad spends much of the year planning its costumes and entertainment. It may be topical, satirical, humorous or just beautiful, but always it is completely different from the year before. Head of the whole celebration is the Guizer Jarl, and each year he tries to outdo every other Up-Helly-A' ever held before.

Following the spectacular climax of the torchlight parade, the town hall, schools, hotels, lodges and other public buildings are thrown open for feasting and dancing.

But, ah, that climax! Every year a faithful 30-foot replica of a Viking ship is built by the "Dock Boys," volunteer carpenters. Flanked and followed by the torchbearing guizers, the Guizer Jarl is towed through the parade route in the galley. At the end comes the ship's Valhalla. The Jarl takes his leave of the ship, the guizers encircle the vessel, the "Galley Song" is sung, cheers are called and raised. Then, at the command of the Jarl and a bugle call, 800 torchbearers hurl their flaming torches into the ship. As the flames roar skyward they sing "The Norseman's Home" and within minutes the squads are moving toward the halls where hosts and hostesses are waiting.

A permanent Up-Helly-A' longship was completed in 1980. It participates in neighboring festivities but in no way affects the burning of the elaborate model each year. (There is an intriguing hint of some colorful history in this note in the 1981 program: "A real sea-going galley had been the dream of successive Up-Helly-A' committees through the years, which came nearest to fruition when a galley-load of Vikings boarded the cruise liner *Viceroy of India* in Lerwick Harbor in 1932. In the light of their experience the exercise was not repeated....")

Each year the reigning Jarl chooses to represent a specific Viking or early Norse hero. There have been Frithiof, Leif Eriksson, Erik the Red, Torf-Einar, King Magnus Barelegs, Olaf the Saint and many others. In recent years Jarls have searched history to come up with Norsemen directly associated with Shetland. In 1982 Jarl Kenneth Crossan chose King Haakon, having learned that the king, while on that fateful journey that ended in the sea fight at Largs, had put into Bressay Sound.

In his memoirs, the late historian Arthur Laurenson theorizes that while anchored there the king would have rowed in to have a conversation with the local farm owner. Whether or not he actually set foot on the site where Lerwick was later built, one thing is certain:

"....that for many days he was in what is now its harbour and he must have rowed upon its waters. In his scarlet kirtle, and wrapped in his boat cloak, with his gold-hilted sword girt round him, we can see the figure which six-hundred years ago played a great part in the history of the North."

The Pacific and Orient cruise ships go from Aberdeen to Lerwick. There is also air service, which also connects Lerwick with the Orkney Islands.

Explore!
Europe's Nomads

*"Ulvkel and Arnkel and Gye, they made
here a Thing-place."*
      Ballsta Thing-Place, Uppland

They are the last of Europe's nomads, the Lapplanders or *Samer,* who inhabit the far north areas of the Scandinavian peninsula. They are a fabled people whose existence has been known to scholars almost since the time of Christ, but they are still a puzzle to us in many ways.

They live on the north reaches of four lands — Norway, Sweden, Finland and the USSR. With their old migratory life barely surviving, their existence today would make a fascinating study. For example, today's reindeer herder, going from his winter residence to the summer camp, is likely to fly in, especially if the area is very remote. If nearer to civilization, he will probably take a pickup.

But still much of the old culture remains, and many persons in Scandinavia are helping the Lapps to keep alive their old crafts especially. Sami handcraft takes many of its designs from relics that are thousands of years old. Sami designs are recognizable on 10,000-year old rock carvings in Scandinavia and the Kola peninsula. Their *duodji* today is part of that old tradition, executed in clothing, wood, horn, leather and pewter work. Many Swedish designs have been influenced by Sami art.

When the Roman historian Tacitus wrote about them in 98 A.D., these were an almost mythical people. Tacitus called them the *Fenni,* who lived even further north than the Germanic tribes. Plinius the Elder called their region *Ultima Thule,* and the inhabitants have been known variously through the years as the people of the Thule, Fennea Seritfinnia, Finnmarchia, Lappia and Lappland. The Lapps themselves call their land *Sameatnam. (Same* means Lapp and *nam* land). They call themselves the *Samer,* and speak of *Sami* culture.

"Scritofini" was a term used by one 8th century historian for them. *Scrito* meant "to run," and the name evolved from the way the people, men and women alike, ran over the snow on curved pieces of wood, pursuing wild beasts.

At the end of the 9th century, a wealthy Norwegian named Ottar sailed from Halogaland for a visit with the English king, Alfred the Great. Here scribes wrote down all he had to tell them about the people he called the *Finnas,* or *Fenner.* Ottar had made a journey far north into their lands, and he also had *Fenner* working for him, tending 600 reindeer on his vast holdings where he raised horses, cattle, sheep and pigs as well. The *Fenner* added to Ottar's tidy income, for he collected taxes from them in the form of reindeer, skins, barrels of feathers and ship's ropes of whale and seal skin.

The origin of the Lapps has been debated for centuries.

At the time Tacitus wrote about them, they inhabited all of Finland. But they were pushed north as the people who were to become the Finns pushed up from the south. It is generally agreed the Lapps are related to the Finns and Samoyeds. Their language belongs to the Uralic family of languages, as does Finnish.

But others argue that they are a race in themselves. Are they descendants of a polar race, a race that was the origin of the dwarfs of mythology? No, said others, their language indicated they had had no contact with the Scandinavians until the beginning of the Iron Age, and that they must have followed the receding land ice north and west from the Ural mountains.

In all of Scandinavia, only the Lapps may own reindeer.

Then discovery of a paleolithic culture on the Arctic seacoast indicated the area was inhabited by humans through the Ice Age. Driven by the ice, they must have taken refuge along the Norwegian Sea. These, said some anthropologists, must have been "proto-Lapps," forbears of the Lapps. Driven first to the coast, they must have followed the receding ice inland.

Some believe there are two distinct types within the Lapp race. For the most part they are short people, up to our shoulders, with short legs, often bowed legs. Their hair is dark, but there are also blonde Lapps and some tall Lapps.

There are as many as 50 separate dialects among the Lapps. And there are almost as many variations in the styles of caps they wear! For while the Lapp clothing is basic — a tunic of fur, coat, trousers, laced shoes — there are as many as ten variations on just one traditonal style of man's cap, and as many or more for women.

Explore!

Rubbing to preserve

"These brothers were the best of men
at home and abroad on expeditions.
They maintained their retinue well.
Thorstein fell in battle east in Russia,
army leader, best of landsmen."

Stone at Turinge, Södermanland

If you've toured cathedrals abroad, you've no doubt seen people on their knees industriously rubbing away with a piece of graphite on white paper.

But you needn't travel back to the land of your ancestors to enjoy making rubbings of some historic surface that will remind you of your ties with the past.

Even on a trip to the area where your immigrant ancestors settled, you can find things of interest to copy through this medium.

There are gravestones in old cemeteries. There may be an ornamental doorplate in the old church your grandparents attended, a dedicatory plate in a stained glass window, cornerstones in buildings that bear a family name, historical markers in a park or on a landmark building.

Rubbing is a simple process but it takes a little practice to develop the right hand pressure. It is done by placing (and securing lightly with tape) a piece of paper or cloth over the surface and rubbing or dabbing with such media as colored waxes, inks or graphite. It's an old method of documentation that began in China, then moved to Japan, Cambodia, Thailand, Europe and the rest of the world. It's an art that children, too, can enjoy doing.

A woman who has conducted many "city rubbing" workshops has published a book that explains exactly how it's done. "Rubbing Craft" may be ordered directly from the author, Cecily Barth Firestein, 8 East 96th Street, New York, N.Y. 10028.

In her book Ms. Firestein demonstrates how rubbings can be translated into patterns for needlepoint, latch-hook rugs, stencils, silkscreen art, jewelry, T-shirts, pillows and the like.

Explore!

The Girl with the Horn

*"For Birging her brother cut
these runes; my dear sister,
be good to me."*

Opedal runestone, Hardanger

Together with the Viking ship and the red horse, the figure of a girl blowing a long horn has become a familiar figure for Scandinavian ventures. You'll find her in painted designs and needlepoint patterns. Many assume it's a herd girl calling her cows or goats.

But the courageous young Guri is very much a part of Norwegian history.

The year was 1612. Since Norway was ruled by Danish King Christian IV and since Christian had gone to war agaisnt Sweden, every young, able-bodied Norwegian man was off in army service that summer.

In July of that summer Guri, a beautiful young girl who was engaged to her soldier sweetheart, Kjell, visited the isolated old stave church on File Mountain in south-central Norway. Here a holy man told her and her lover, "From the West will come white boats bearing red-clad men, that will be the worse for you both."

Within a month, Scottish ships sailed into Romsdalfjord, bringing an army of some 800 mercenaries under the command of Col. George Sinclair of Scotland. A ruthless warrior, he had agreed to command a company of Scottish soldiers under hire to the Swedish king. His assignment was to cross Norway and reach the Swedish border. But even before he set foot on Norwegian soil a new plan possessed him: to conquer this largely rural land for himself and set himself up as king.

Traveling through Romsdal and the rich valley of Gudbrandsdal, the band looted, pillaged, raped, killed and burned their way from farm to farm.

Guri, the story goes, barely escaped death when the invaders murdered her foster family.

At last the farmers who were left in the region managed to get together a body of defenders. At Kringen, in Vreden Parish in Sel, was a mountain pass with a lake on one side and steep rock walls on the other. Sinclair would have to pass this way. Here they built their defense — an enormous wall of logs and boulders, held together with stout ropes. Poles supported

149

more rock and debris, all fashioned to release with the cut of a single rope. The avalanche was calculated to crush the Scots in the narrow pass.

To young Guri fell the assignment of rowing out to a small island in the lake, taking with her a *lur,* a musical horn fashioned from a buck's horn. (Also called a *prillar,* it accounts for the name "Prillar Guri," literally "The Horn Girl.") Here she blew on her horn and waved her kerchief as the Scots approached.

The first vanguard was allowed to pass. Then, following a shot that felled Sinclair, the avalanche was loosed. In the melee that followed, the Scots were all but wiped out. Only 18 remained alive to be captured and taken to Copenhagen.

But to the courageous Guri it was a hollow victory. Her beloved Kjell, on leave from the army, died in the battle.

~~~~~~

It was at Kringen where local farmers and peasants took up positions and waited for Prillar Guri to sound the alarm as the Scots approached. Today the provincial dress of this region resembles a Scottish tartan. It is not the Sinclair tartan, but is close to the McAlister. At that time in Scotland clan tartans had not been developed, but there were regional tartans.

~~~~~~

Sinclair's grave is marked at Kvam churchyard, and the infamous date of August 26, 1612, is part of Norwegian history.

A fictionalized story of the Scottish invasion appeared in an Oslo newspaper some years ago. It has been translated by Marvel deSordi and Arthur Stavig, and follows the marauders through Bjorli, Lesjaskog, Lesja, Bottheim, Tofte, Dovre and Laurgard. It's a fascinating tale and a "must" for anyone wanting to learn more about Norwegian history. The book, "Prillar Guri, A Heroine of Old Norway," is available from Stavig Enterprises, 12808 N. E. 120th Street, Kirkland, Washington 98033.

If one of the needlecraft shops in your area carries Scandinavian designs, you may be able to bring the story alive by working a beautiful wall hanging of the "girl with the horn."

Explore!
More unusual foods

"A man generous with his
food and eloquent."

- The Vappeby stone, Uppland

The Scandinavian foods mentioned in this book are barely a hint of the variety of foods you can find that are peculiar to Scandinavia, past or present.

Why not make a collection of your own? Begin by asking older Scandinavian friends to give you old-time recipes they remember. Research old church cookbooks. Write to the embassies and trade offices of the various Scandinavian countries — some have food booklets available.

Here's one for a start. Would you like to know how to make goat cheese? After all, travelers to Norway are always being urged, "Bring me back some real goat cheese!"

Ekte gjetost, real goat cheese, is rarer than it used to be since dairy farming in Norway is much more popular than goat farming. There are good cheeses made from a blend of goat and cow milk, like low-fat "magerost" and "Gudbrandsdalost." But sometimes high in the mountains of Norway you'll see a small sign, *"Gjetost."* It is made on some farms simply to keep alive the old traditions and maintain a high quality.

Thanks to the Tourist Magazine of Western Norway, here is a recipe for the rich, mahogany-colored cheese that would have been made on the farms in times past:

To get 20 pounds of cheese, you'd begin with 50 gallons of goat milk. (Come back, come back, we didn't say you had to make it!) Heated to 40 degrees centigrade, the milk separates into 80 quarts of skim milk and 20 quarts of cream. The cream is skimmed off.

When the skim milk reaches 50 degrees, two tablespoons of rennet are added and the mixture is left until it "sets." Now the mixture must be put into another large vat and warmed until the curds and whey separate. These go into separate vats. When the curds are heated to 80 degrees, the milk albumen also separates; this is removed and mixed with the whey for another cheese product.

Now the cream goes back into the curds and is simmered again. The simmering and stirring goes on for seven hours, during the last two of which the mixture must be kept moving constantly. You must begin stirring it again after it has been poured into a smaller vat and the cooling begins. In fact, it is stirred until it is almost solid and only then is it packed into forms to harden for a couple of days.

Comments the writer: "Not exactly a beginner's recipe!"

Maybe you'd rather start with rice pudding?

In Conclusion

In a poem written to Georg Brandes, the great Norwegian playwright Henrik Ibsen wondered why modern man was so oppressed by restlessness and apathy. And while he didn't answer his own question in the poem, Ibsen let the answer come alive again and again in his plays: the problem is our willingness to let ourselves be dominated by the past.

That willingness, as he put it, is "a corpse in the cargo." He was referring, of course, to the habit of sailors who, when things went very badly at sea, would say, "There is a corpse in the cargo."

When we look backward in time, as we've done in this book, we run the risk of putting ourselves into that school of thought against which Ibsen railed through most of his career. Norway at that time was becoming acutely, sentimentally aware of her roots. All that was old, romantic, traditional, peasant and folk-oriented held center stage in literature, art and the theatre.

Into that milieu came the controversial Ibsen, his characters striding squarely into the present, emphasizing personal freedom, speaking freedom of thought and conscience.

In our own time, as never before in history, man is compelled to look the present squarely in the eye if he is to survive. Because we face such consuming issues and problems, we cannot afford to treat a nostalgic look at our past as an end. An appreciation of the past can only be a means toward understanding what is good in it and what is not, and what can be applied to our own existence.

The Scandinavians, both as individuals and nations, have learned to be fiercely independent while at the same time willing to show cooperation. They have, again both as individuals and as nations, developed a rugged stubbornness to say "no" to outside interests that would change them, but again and again they have shown unfettered compassion. They are proud of the traditions that make them unique, separate from each other; they are even more proud of the heritage and traits that unite them. Idealistic, they are also tolerant.

We face problems our forefathers never heard of: pollution, overpopulation, global hunger and above all, the threat of nuclear annihilation of civilization as we know it. And too many of us are still carrying the corpse in the cargo, trying to treat today's problems with yesterday's solutions. New solutions demand daring and a sense of adventure.

If we can draw strength from our forefathers' struggles, if we can recognize their mistakes in order not to be dominated by them, perhaps then we will find that same daring that sent them out into the great Atlantic — Leif, Thorvaldr, Thorfinn, Gudridr, Helgi, Finnbogi and all the rest — yes, and Great Grandfather and Great Grandmother as well!

Bibliography

In addition to books mentioned specifically in the text, some of the following have been used by the author in preparation of this book. Others are simply recommended for your pleasure and for learning more about the Scandinavians.

JOHANNES BRONDSTED, "The Vikings." Penguin Books, New York, N.Y., 1965.

JAMES GRAHAM-CAMPBELL, "The Viking World." Ticknor & Fields, 1980.

ELIZABETH JANEWAY, "The Vikings." Random House, New York, 1951.

GWYN JONES, "A History of the Vikings." Oxford University Press, London.

OLE KLINDT-JENSEN, "A History of Scandinavian Archaeology." Thames & Hudson, Ltd., London, 1975.

DAVID M. WILSON, "The Vikings and Their Origin." A & W Publishers, Inc., New York, 1980.

JOHN BAUER, "Great Swedish Fairy Tales." Delacorte-Seymour and Dell Publishing.

INGRI and EDGAR PARIN D'AULAIRE, "The Terrible Troll Bird." Doubleday and Co., Inc., Garden City, N.Y., 1976. Also by D'Aulaire: "D'Aulaire's Trolls," "Leif the Lucky," "Nils," "Ola," "Norse Gods and Giants."

INGA HACK, "Danish Fairy Tales." Follett Publishing Co., Chicago and New York, 1964.

"Fairy Tales Told in Sweden" and "Fairy Tales Told in Denmark," Little Brown and Co.

HANNA ASTRUP LARSEN, "Denmark's Best Stories." W. W. Norton & Company, Inc., New York, 1928.

HANNA ASTRUP LARSEN, "Sweden's Best Stories." Books for Libraries Press, Freeport, N.Y., 1928

PETER ANDREAS MUNCH, "Norse Mythology, Legends of Gods and Heroes." The American Scandinavian Foundation, New York, 1927.

O.E. ROLVAAG, "Giants in the Earth." Harper and Row, New York, 1927, 1929.

GEORGE MACAULAY TREVELYAN, "A Shortened History of England." Longmans Green and Co., New York, 1942.

SIGRID UNDSET, "Kristin Lavransdatter, a Triology, 1920, 1921, 1922." 3-volume edition by Alfred A. Knopf, New York, 1946.

JAMES NORBURY, "Traditional Knitting Patterns," 1973.
SIGRID BRIGHT, "Hardanger Embroidery."
FANGLER, WINCKLER & MADSEN, "Danish Pulled Thread Embroidery," 1977.
PAMELA MILLER NESS, "Swedish Tvistsom Embroidery," 1981.
PAMELA MILLER NESS, "Norwegian Smyrna Cross," 1981.
DALE YARN CO., "Knit Your Own Norwegian Sweaters," 1974.

INGA ARNO BERG and GUNNEL HAZELIUS BERG, "Folkdrakter." ICA bokforlag Vasteras (Sweden), 1975.

AAGOT NOSS, "Adolph Tidemand og folk han motte." (Norske folkedrakter) Universitets forlaget (Norway), 1981.

Books from Dillon Press, Minneapolis:
LILY LORENZEN, "Of Swedish Ways."
MAC HAFFIE and NIELSEN, "Of Danish Ways."
AINI RAJANEN, "Of Finnish Ways."
BENT VANBERG, "Of Norwegian Ways."

HELEN ELIZABETH BLANK, "The Flowers of Dalarna" (Swedish floral painting), 1975.
INGA PETERSON, "Rosemaling Technique," 1966.
TRUDY SONDROL WASSON, Old Rogaland Rosemaling, Oelwein, Iowa, 1983.
VILHELM MOBERG (CARL ARTUR VILHELM MOBERG), "The Emigrants." Simon & Schuster, New York, 1951, "Unto a Good Land." Simon & Schuster, New York, 1954; "When I Was a Child." Alfred A. Knopf, New York, 1956; "The Earth Is Ours," a trilogy, Simon & Schuster, New York, 1940.
CARL-ERIK JOHANSSON, "Cradled in Sweden." Everton Publishers, Inc., Logan, Utah, 1972.
JAMES ROBERT ENTERLINE, "Viking America." Doubleday & Co., Garden City, N.Y., 1972.
ROBERT A. HALL, JR., "The Kensington Rune Stone Is Genuine." Hornbeam Press, Columbia, S.C., 1982.
HJALMAR R. HOLAND, "Explorations in America Before Columbus." Twayne Publishers, Inc., New York, 1956.
HJALMAR R. HOLAND, "A Holy Mission to Minnesota 600 Years Ago," Parkridge, 1959.
FREDERICK POHL, "Atlantic Crossings Before Columbus." W. W. Norton .. Company, Inc., New York, 1961.
FREDERICK J. POHL, "The Lost Discovery." W. W. Norton .. Company, Inc., New York.
FREDERICK J. POHL, "The Viking Explorers." Thomas Crowell Co., 1966.
EDWARD REMAN, "The Norse Discoveries and Explorations in America." University of California Press, Berkeley and Los Angeles, 1949.

MARM and SOMMERFELT, "Norwegian." The English Universities Press, Ltd., London, 1967.

EINAR HAUGEN, "Beginning Norwegian." Appleton-Century-Crofts, Inc., New York.

GAVAN DAVIS, "Shoal of Time." University Press of Hawaii, Honolulu, 1968.

ANDREW W. LIND, "An Island Community." Greenwood Press, New York, 1968.

ERNEST MANKER, "People of Eight Seasons." AB Nordbok, Gothenburg (Sweden), 1975.

ASBJORN NESHEIM, "Introducing the Lapps." J. D. Tanum, 1963.

NORAH GOURLIE, "A Winter With Finnish Lapps." Blackie and Sons, Ltd., 1939.

NANCY HEDLUND, "Swedish Cultural Coloring Book."

Coloring books by CATHERINE A. MACARO, "Sweden," "Norway," "Finland," "Denmark."

The following books are required reading in Professor Birgitta Steene's course in Scandinavian Children's Literature at the University of Washington:

"East of the Sun and West of the Moon"
"Great Swedish Fairy Tales"
"Tales and Stories of Hans Christian Andersen"
Elsa Beskow's "Pelle's New Suit"
Astrid Lindgren's "Pippi Longstocking"
Maria Gripe's "The Glassblower's Children"
Tove Jansson's "Moomin Family"

The following books are recommended reading for the course. All are in English.

Hans Aanrud, "Sidel Longskirt" (from the Norwegian)
Ottilia Adelborg, "Clean Peter and the Children at Grubbylea" (Swedish)
W. Bodekker, "It's Raining, said Jon Twaining," Danish Nursery Rhymes (Danish)
Nils Olof Franzen, "Children of the Moor" (Swedish)
Selma Lagerlof, "The Wonderful Adventures of Nils" (Swedish)
Maj Lindman, "Snipp, Snapp, Snurr and the Buttered Bread" (Swedish)
Carl Larsson, "A Home" (Swedish)
Anna Loken, "When the Sun Danced" (Norwegian)
Jeanna Oterdahl, "April Adventure" (Swedish)
Barbra Ring, "Peik" (Norwegian)
Inger and Lasse Sandberg, "Nicholas' Favorite Pet" (Swedish)
Jens Sigegaard, "Palle alene i verden" (Danish)
Edith Unnerstad, "Saucepan Journey" (Swedish)

Index

Introduction 7

The Vikings 9

An Abbreviated History 23

Folk Tales, Folk Lore 29

    Hans Christian Anderson 38

    The Gods of Legend 41

The Tomtes of Hellerup 42

    The Christmas Rose 44

The Home Arts 45

    Woodcarving 48

    Painting 50

    Weaving 52

    Embroidery 57

    Knitting 62

    Straw Weaving 63

Folk Costumes 65

    To Acquire Your Own Costume 71

    Isolation and Travel 75

Music and Dance 77

Holidays 81

Favored Foods 91

The Great Emigration 105
Tracing Your Ancestry............................115
What's In a Name? 121
Explore Further..................................125
    The World of Museums.......................126
    Before Columbus............................132
    Speaking the Language 137
    Norwegians in Hawaii 137
    The Biggest Viking Festivals................143
    Europe's Nomads 146
    Rubbing to Preserve 148
    The Girl With the Horn 150
    More Unusual Foods 152

Conclusion 153
Bibliography....................................154